British Literature

Excellence in Literature: English 4

Fourth Edition

Janice Campbell

Everyday Education

Making time for things that matter.

Excellence in Literature: Reading and Writing through the Classics
— Introduction to Literature (English I)
— Literature and Composition (English II)
— American Literature: A Survey Course (English III)
— **British Literature: A Survey Course (English IV)**
— World Literature: A Survey Course (English V)
— The Complete Curriculum (All 5 years in a binder)
— Excellence in Literature *Handbook for Writers*

Fourth Edition: © 2021 Everyday Education, LLC

Everyday Education, LLC
P. O. Box 549
Ashland, VA 23005
www.EverydayEducation.com

Front Cover Art: *Landscape with the Fall of Icarus* by Pieter Bruegel the Elder (c. 1590)
Index of context resource links:

  https://excellence-in-literature.com/curriculum-user-content/e4-context-resources/.

Campbell, Janice

British Literature / Excellence in literature: reading and writing through the classics / Janice Campbell

ISBN: 978-1-61322-076-4

1. Literature—Explication. 2. Literature—History and Criticism. 3. Books and reading. I. Title.

It is a great thing to start life with a small number of

really good books

which are your very own.

You may not appreciate them at first.

You may pine for your novel of crude and unadulterated adventure.

You may, and will, give it the preference when you can.

But the dull days come, and the rainy days come,

and always you are driven to fill up the chinks of your reading

with the worthy books which wait so patiently for your notice.

And then suddenly, on a day which marks an epoch in your life,

you understand the difference.

You see, like a flash, how the one stands for nothing,

and the other for literature.

From that day onwards you may return to your crudities,

but at least you do so with some

standard of comparison in your mind.

You can never be the same as you were before.

Then gradually the good thing becomes more dear to you;

it builds itself up with your growing mind;

it becomes a part of your better self, and so,

at last, you can look, as I do now, at the old covers

and love them for all that they have meant in the past.

—Arthur Conan Doyle, *Through the Magic Door*

Thank you!

I would like to offer special thanks to some of my former students,
who graciously agreed to share their work as models.

Erin Bensing

Jonathan Bensing

Lindsey Bensing

Eric Lansing

Rebecca Shealy-Houghton

Jesse Thompson

I would also like to thank the helpers who have contributed time and expertise to
make Excellence in Literature and the accompanying website what they are today.

Taylor Campbell

Rebecca Shealy-Houghton

Craig Campbell

Andrew Bailey

"In ordinary life,
we hardly realize that we receive a great deal more than we give,

and that it is only with gratitude that life becomes rich."

Dietrich Bonhoeffer

Deo gratias.

Contents

Preface

Dear Student,

Do you know that very few people know how to read?

It is not that they cannot decipher words on a page, but they simply do not know how to place what they read into its proper literary and historical context. They may understand WHAT happened in a story, but they do not know WHY. They may feel strongly about the story, yet they never stop to wonder WHY they feel as they do, or HOW the author made it happen.

If you are wondering why you should care about the HOW and WHY of literature, think about it like this: Reading without understanding is like walking onto a softball field and batting the ball, without any knowledge of what to do next. You may hit the ball out of the park, but if you do not run the bases and complete the play, you have missed the whole point of the activity.

It is the same with reading. In order to complete the process, it is necessary to think deeply about what you read. Reading is a conversation between a reader and a writer. The author creates a world, peoples it with characters, and presents a story. The reader enters the author's world, meets the characters, and follows the story line. When you write about literature, as you will this year, the conversation shifts. It becomes a dialogue between you, as an analytical reader and writer, and the reader of your essay.

In this literature curriculum, I'll introduce you to "deep reading," in which you will immerse in a great story, contemplating as you read. In each module, I'll point you toward additional resources such as poetry, art, music, and history. These things will help you understand a bit more about the author, his or her time and place in history, and the cultural influences that shaped the work of literature you are studying.

You will find that you like some books and authors better than others, just as I do. Each novel, poem, essay, or play in this literature series has been carefully chosen for its quality and its place in the panorama of literary history. Even if you find you don't enjoy a particular work as much as another, it has been included because it has something important to convey. One thing you will discover is that sometimes the stories you like least stick with you the longest and sometimes even teach you the most.

I love to read, and I am happy to have the opportunity to share some of my favorite great books with you. Some will make you laugh, others may make you cry, but above all, I hope they make you think. When you finish your reading for the year, I know your mind will be more richly furnished than when you began, and that is a very good thing.

Janice Campbell

www.ExcellenceInLiterature.com

P. S. As you read through this study guide and all the books in EIL, you will most likely encounter words you do not know. I'm sure you know what to do when this happens. Look it up and write down the word and its definition, and you will be expanding your vocabulary without much effort at all!

Overview and Objectives

*In the case of good books, the point is not to see how many of them you can get through,
but rather how many can get through to you.*

—Mortimer J. Alder

Excellence in Literature (EIL) is a college-preparatory course of study. It is my goal to

- Introduce you to great literature from the Western literary tradition.

- Teach you to read with discernment.

- Help you become an independent, self-motivated learner.

- Provide tools you can use to strengthen your writing skills.

- Introduce you to sources for high-quality online and off-line research.

- Prepare you for college classes by expecting you to turn in carefully researched, well-considered writing assignments in the assigned format, with preliminary proofreading completed.

In the five levels of this literature series, you will be reading some of the greatest works of literature ever written. They are great not just because they are technically well done, though that certainly is a factor, but also because they reveal truth through the power of story.

EIL uses great literature, studied in its historic, literary, and artistic contexts, to help you learn to think and write analytically. This book is designed for you, the student, to use independently, so it contains specific instructions for each assignment, and a suggested schedule, as well as the references you need in order to do the background reading and research for each module.

You may be surprised to find I have not provided a lengthy introduction and a lot of background material for each book and author. This is because you have reached the age when you can assume responsibility for learning. Rather than spoon-feeding you basic, easily-researched information (and having you zone out in the middle of paragraph two), I have pointed you to resources and links that will enable you to perform the contextual research needed to more deeply understand the focus text. This is similar to the kind of research you will do for college courses, so if you learn how to do it now, you should be quite good at it by the time you graduate.

How to Benefit from This Guide

There are three main sections in this study guide. Begin by reading the front and back sections first, as they will explain how to use the curriculum. Here's what you will find in each section.

Section I: How to Use the Curriculum

In the first section, you will find an explanation of how EIL works, suggestions for how to create a study routine and organize your study materials, chapters on how to read analytically and how to write essays.

Section II: Modules

Following this you will find the syllabus section, with a study outline and schedule for each module.

Section III: How to Format and Grade Papers

In the final section you will find instructions for writing specific types of papers, information for your writing mentor on how to evaluate papers, and sample papers that demonstrate correct MLA format (if you do not know what that is, be patient—it is explained in the samples and the glossary). Be sure to read all the chapters so you can be successful as you work through the assignments.

Scheduling

Each level of EIL has nine modules. Each module is intended to be completed in four relatively brief, but intense, weeks. Your writing mentor can adapt that schedule for you if needed.

You may choose to group the modules into a traditional nine-month school year, or to use a four weeks on, one week off schedule. For a weekly routine, our family loosely followed a college-style block schedule in which we studied the humanities (literature, history, art, and music) in 2- to 3 hour blocks of time on Tuesday and Thursday; and math, science, and related subjects on Monday and Wednesday, but you are free to do what works best for you and your family.

Each assignment has been carefully chosen and scheduled so that knowledge and skills can build cumulatively, even if your writing mentor changes the order in which you study the modules. It is important that you learn time management skills that will help you complete assignments with minimal stress. If you are working with a writing mentor such as your parent, a writing evaluator, a coach, or a co-op instructor, be sure to agree in advance on a schedule, so that you can plan your work efficiently. Above all, do not spend three weeks procrastinating; then try to cram the assigned reading and writing into one week. Believe me, it does not work!

Course Format

Excellence in Literature courses focus in depth on selected great authors or literary movements, while exploring the context of the author's life and working through additional reading and writing. You'll be able to practice writing in a number of different formats, and to grow thoroughly familiar with some of the greatest writers and literary works of all time.

Audio Books

Although many students are visual learners and do well reading each novel, auditory or kinesthetic learners may benefit from listening to unabridged audio versions of some of the focus texts. Any of the epic poems such as *Beowulf* or *Odyssey* work especially well in audio, as that is how they were enjoyed by the original audiences. It can also be easier to appreciate the rhythm and cadence of the language when you are listening to a good reader. The goal is for you to thoroughly understand and enjoy the material we cover, so use the learning tools that work best for you.

Context Materials

For each module there will be "context resources"—history, art, poetry, and more — to read, listen to, or watch. These will help you understand the focus work. You'll find links to interesting and informative websites, and recommendations for additional readings. Many of these are hosted or linked at Excellence-in-Literature. com; you can view them at the "Study Guide Links" pages on the site.

Do not feel limited by these resource suggestions. I encourage you to find and include other resources, such as videos, field trips, or other useful books. The more rich and varied the context materials, the more you'll learn about the focus text. If you find a book or author you particularly enjoy, take the time to read more of his or her writings and others like them. EIL is a solid foundation, and it is designed to be flexible, so you can shape it to reflect your own interests.

Study Clusters

You may want to consider planning the high school years in study clusters—grouping American history with American literature, British history with British literature, and so forth. This reinforces learning and increases memorable context for both literature and history. You may mix and match EIL modules to fit the history you are studying, though it is wise to remember that the modules graduate in difficulty through the five levels of the curriculum.

The Honors Track

In each module, you will find additional reading suggestions under the "Honors" heading. If you would like to earn an honors-level grade (weighted by .5 grade point), you need to read an extra book and usually do summary titles and an approach paper for each module. At the end of the school year, you will also write an additional research paper, which is assigned in the Honors chapter. This will complete the honors track.

To earn advanced placement or college credit for the class (weighted by 1.0 grade point), you will also need to take an AP or CLEP exam. You can find complete details on how to assign weighted grades and record advanced classes in my book, *Transcripts Made Easy* (www.TranscriptsMadeEasy.com). Additional information about how and why to earn college credits can be found in *Get a Jump Start on College!* (www.GetAJumpStartOnCollege.com).

Excellence in Literature: Reading and Writing through the Classics

Prerequisites for Success

Excellence in Literature is intended for use by students in grades 8–12. For each level, you are expected to have age-appropriate skills in grammar, spelling, and language mechanics. You should grammar- and spell-check all papers and refer to a writer's handbook to check your grammar, style, and punctuation before turning in your papers. Learning to self-edit is part of the writing process, and it helps to learn it before you arrive at college or the world of work.

If you have not done much literary analysis or essay writing before EIL, there are a couple of resources you might find helpful. *Teaching the Classics* by Adam and Missy Andrews is a brief DVD course that teaches literary analysis using short works to illustrate the principles and methods. For essay writing, you can use the EIL *Handbook for Writers* recommended to accompany these study guides. If you need an additional resource, *The Elegant Essay Writing Lessons* by Lesha Myers is a solid guide. Either resource can be used concurrently with *Excellence in Literature.*

Learning Philosophy

Learn (lûrn) v. 1 Acquire knowledge of (a subject) or skill in (an art, etc.) as a result of study, experience, or instruction; acquire or develop an ability to do. 4.1 Commit to memory.

—Oxford Shorter English Dictionary

Part of the foundation of the *Excellence in Literature* philosophy is the verb "learn." Learning is an active endeavor, and the main action takes place in one person—the learner. That's you! In this course you'll receive not only knowledge, but you'll also learn to become an active learner. You'll take away study methods and communication skills you can use for many subjects. There is great joy in learning, and this, above all, is what I want to communicate.

The Learning Process: Roles of Excellence in Literature, the Student, and the Writing Mentor

The EIL guide will

- Establish the scope and sequence for the class.
- Assign appropriate readings.
- Provide a suggested schedule for assignments.
- Provide time management and organization tips.
- Provide a rubric for objectively evaluating completed assignments.

The Student will

- Study this book and understand the sequence and timing of assignments.
- Ask questions of the writing mentor when something is not clearly understood.
- Actively seek to learn from each assignment.
- Complete all assignments on time.
- Make no excuses.
- Enjoy great literature.

The Writing Mentor (teacher or parent) will

- Help the student obtain required books and reference materials.
- Verify that assignments are completed on schedule.
- Use the rubric or select a qualified writing evaluator to provide feedback for the student.
- Provide an evaluation summary for the year, using the form found at the end of this book.

Module 4.1 Suggested Schedule

Beowulf

Concepts and Ideas	Writing Types	Poetry
• Characteristics of epic poetry • Concept of the heroic ideal	• Kennings activity • Historical Approach Paper • Retelling OR Essay	• "Reading Poetry" section in the "How to Read a Book" chapter. • Caedmon • Other Anglo-Saxon poets

Week	What to Read	What to Write	Honors Reading (optional)	Honors Writing (optional)
1	❏ Module 4.1 in Study Guide ❏ Begin reading and/or listening to *Beowulf* ❏ Context Resources	❏ Record and define kennings from the text		
2	❏ Finish *Beowulf* ❏ Finish context resources	❏ Historical Approach Paper	❏ *The Dream of the Rood* OR ❏ *Caedmon's Hymn* OR *The Battle of Maldon*	❏ Summary titles ❏ Approach paper
3		❏ Write the first draft of a 750-word paper. 　❏ Use the rubric to check your paper 　❏ Proofread out loud 　❏ Turn it in for evaluation		
4	Additional reading ❏ Compare/Contrast Essay Instructions (F&M chapter)	❏ Revise your draft based on the rubric and evaluation comments. ❏ Finish, proofread, and turn in your paper.		

Notes:
• You will find complete assignment instructions in the Assignment Schedule for this module.
• The suggested schedule may be adapted to fit your needs; just check off each assignment as you complete it.

Canterbury Tales

Concepts and Ideas	Writing Types	Poetry
• Framed narrative • Middle English	• Author profile • Letter from a character • Compare/Contrast Essay	• Dante Alighieri

Week	What to Read	What to Write	Honors Reading (optional)	Honors Writing (optional)
1	❏ Module 4.2 in Study Guide ❏ Start reading the *Canterbury Tales* ❏ Start Context Resources	❏ Author Profile		
2	❏ Finish reading *Canterbury Tales* ❏ Continue Context resources	❏ Letter from a character		

3	❏ Finish reading, watching, and listening to context resources.	❏ Write first draft of a 750-word paper
		  ❏ Use the rubric to check your essay or letter
		  ❏ Proofread out loud
		  ❏ Turn it in for evaluation
			❏ *Piers Plowman*	For your chosen works, write
				❏ Summary titles
				❏ Approach paper

4	Additional reading	❏ Revise your draft based on the rubric and evaluation comments. ❏ Finish, proofread, and turn in your paper.		

Notes:
• You will find complete assignment instructions in the Assignment Schedule for this module.
• The Additional Reading recommendations can be found at Excellence-in-Literature.com; use the site search box to go to it.
• The suggested schedule may be adapted to fit your needs; just check off each assignment as you complete it.

Module 4.3 Suggested Schedule

Spenser, Gawain, and the Arthurian Legend

Concepts and Ideas	Writing Types	Poetry
• Chivalry and honor • Characters and motifs across the centuries • Allegory	• Author profile • Approach Paper • Copy Epigraphs • Literary OR Poetry Analysis Essay OR • Rewrite in prose	• Alfred, Lord Tennyson

Week	What to Read	What to Write	Honors Reading (optional)	Honors Writing (optional)
1	❑ Module 4.3 in Study Guide ❑ Start reading the focus works ❑ Start Context Resources	❑ Author Profile	❑ *Le Morte d'Arthur*	❑ Summary titles ❑ Approach paper
2 3	❑ Continue reading the focus works; finish if possible. ❑ Continue Context resources	❑ Approach Paper ❑ Copy epigraphs		

	❑ Finish reading, watching, and listening to context resources.	❑ Write first draft of a 750-word essay or prose rewrite
		❑ Use the rubric to check your essay
		  ❑ Proofread out loud
		  ❑ Turn it in for evaluation		

4	Additional reading ❑	❑ Revise your draft based on the rubric and evaluation comments. ❑ Finish, proofread, and turn in your paper.		

Notes:
• You will find complete assignment instructions in the Assignment Schedule for this module.
• The suggested schedule may be adapted to fit your needs; just check off each assignment as you complete it.

Module 4.4 Suggested Schedule

King Lear

Concepts and Ideas	Writing Types	Poetry
• Tragedy • Hubris as a catalyst • Fate vs. choice • Purpose of the sub-plot	• Author profile • Scene Summaries • Compare/Contrast Essay	• William Shakespeare • John Donne • Queen Elizabeth I • Sir Walter Raleigh • Sir Philip Sidney • Christopher Marlowe

Week	What to Read	What to Write	Honors Reading (optional)	Honors Writing (optional)
1	❏ Module 4.4 in Study Guide ❏ Start reading *King Lear* ❏ Consider provided questions as you read. ❏ Start Context Resources	❏ Author Profile		
2	❏ Finish *King Lear*; finish if possible ❏ Continue Context resources	❏ Scene summaries	❏ *Hamlet*	❏ Summary titles ❏ Approach paper

3	❏ Finish all reading, watching, and listening to context resources.	❏ Write a first draft of a 750-word essay
		  ❏ Use the rubric to check your paper
		  ❏ Proofread out loud
		  ❏ Turn it in for evaluation		

4	Additional reading	❏ Revise your draft based on the rubric and evaluation comments. ❏ Finish, proofread, and turn in your paper.		

Notes:
• You will find complete assignment instructions in the Assignment Schedule for this module.
• The suggested schedule may be adapted to fit your needs; just check off each assignment as you complete it.

Paradise Lost

Concepts and Ideas	Writing Types	Poetry
• Differences between Medieval and Renaissance epics • Use of classical imagery; allusions • Characteristics of the epic form	• Author profile • Book summaries • Analytical OR Compare/Contrast essay	• John Milton • George Herbert • Andrew Marvell

Week	What to Read	What to Write	Honors Reading (optional)	Honors Writing (optional)
1	❏ Module 4.5 in Study Guide ❏ Start *Paradise Lost* ❏ Start Context Resources	❏ Author profile		
2	❏ Continue reading *Paradise Lost;* finish if possible ❏ Continue Context resources	❏ Book summaries		

3	❏ Finish reading, watching, and listening to context resources.	❏ Write first draft of a 750-word essay
		  ❏ Use the rubric to check your essay
		  ❏ Proofread out loud
		  ❏ Turn it in for evaluation
			❏ *Faust* by Christopher Marlowe OR *Confessions* by St. Augustine	❏ Summary titles
				❏ Approach paper

4	Additional reading ❏	❏ Revise your draft based on the rubric and evaluation comments. ❏ Finish, proofread, and turn in your paper.		

Notes:
• You will find complete assignment instructions in the Assignment Schedule for this module.
• The suggested schedule may be adapted to fit your needs; just check off each assignment as you complete it.

Module 4.6 Suggested Schedule				
Pride and Prejudice				

Concepts and Ideas		**Writing Types**	**Poetry**
• Neoclassical and Romantic period differences • Irony in social commentary		• Author profile • Letters • Essay or Poetry Analysis	• William Blake • Williams Wordsworth • Samuel Taylor Coleridge • Percy Bysshe Shelley • John Keats

Week	What to Read	What to Write	Honors Reading (optional)	Honors Writing (optional)
1	❏ Module 4.6 in Study Guide ❏ Start reading *Pride and Prejudice* ❏ Start Context Resources	❏ Author Profile		
2	❏ Continue *Pride and Prejudice*; finish if possible ❏ Continue Context resources	❏ Letters	❏ *Sense and Sensibility* OR *Middlemarch*	❏ Summary titles ❏ Approach paper

3	❏ Finish reading, watching, and listening to context resources.	❏ Write first draft of a 750-word essay or poetry analysis
		  ❏ Use the rubric to check your essay
		  ❏ Proofread out loud
		  ❏ Turn it in for evaluation		

4	Additional reading	❏ Revise your draft based on the rubric and evaluation comments. ❏ Finish, proofread, and turn in your paper.		

Notes:
• You will find complete assignment instructions in the Assignment Schedule for this module.
• The suggested schedule may be adapted to fit your needs; just check off each assignment as you complete it.

Module 4.7 Suggested Schedule				
Great Expectations				

Concepts and Ideas		**Writing Types**	**Poetry**
• Movement from Romanticism to Realism • Characterization • Paired characters		• Author profile and character list • Historical Approach Paper • Essay	• Elizabeth Barrett Browning • Robert Browning

Week	What to Read	What to Write	Honors Reading (optional)	Honors Writing (optional)
1	❑ Module 4.7 in Study Guide ❑ Begin reading *Great Expectations* ❑ Start Context Resources	❑ Author Profile and character list with personality traits		
2	❑ Finish reading *Great Expectations* ❑ Continue Context resources	❑ Historical Approach Paper	❑ *Oliver Twist* OR *David Copperfield* OR *Vanity Fair*	❑ Summary titles ❑ Approach paper

3	❑ Finish reading, watching, and listening to context resources.	❑ Write first draft of a 750-word paper
		  ❑ Use the rubric to check your paper
		  ❑ Proofread out loud
		  ❑ Turn it in for evaluation		

4	Additional reading	❑ Revise your draft based on the rubric and evaluation comments. ❑ Finish, proofread, and turn in your paper.		

Notes:
• You will find complete assignment instructions in the Assignment Schedule for this module.
• The suggested schedule may be adapted to fit your needs; just check off each assignment as you complete it.

Module 4.8 Suggested Schedule

Wuthering Heights

Concepts and Ideas		Writing Types	Poetry
• Characteristics of Gothic literature • Paired and circular plot elements		• Author profile • Journalistic feature • Analytical or Compare/Contrast Essay	• Emily Brontë • Lord Byron • Samuel Taylor Coleridge

Week	What to Read	What to Write	Honors Reading (optional)	Honors Writing (optional)
1	❏ Module 4.8 in Study Guide ❏ Start reading *Wuthering Heights* ❏ Start Context Resources	❏ Author Profile		
2	❏ Continue reading *Wuthering Heights* ❏ Continue Context resources	❏ Journalistic feature article	❏ *The Tenant of Wildfell Hall* OR ❏ *Jane Eyre* OR ❏ *Frankenstein*	❏ Scene Summaries ❏ Approach paper

3	❏ Finish reading, watching, and listening to context resources.	❏ Write first draft of a 750-word essay
		  ❏ Use the rubric to check your paper
		  ❏ Proofread out loud
		  ❏ Turn it in for evaluation		

4	Additional reading	❏ Revise your draft based on the rubric and evaluation comments. ❏ Finish, proofread, and turn in your paper.		

Notes:
• You will find complete assignment instructions in the Assignment Schedule for this module.
• The suggested schedule may be adapted to fit your needs; just check off each assignment as you complete it.

Excellence in Literature: Reading and Writing through the Classics

	To the Lighthouse			
Concepts and Ideas		**Writing Types**		**Poetry**

To the Lighthouse

Concepts and Ideas	**Writing Types**	**Poetry**
• Characteristics of Modernism • Stream of consciousness • Modernism and happy endings	• Author profile • Approach paper OR Retelling • Literary Analysis Essay	• T. S. Eliot • W. H. Auden • William Butler Yeats • Gerard Manley Hopkins

Week	What to Read	What to Write	Honors Reading (optional)	Honors Writing (optional)
1	❏ Module 4.9 in Study Guide ❏ Start reading *To the Lighthouse* ❏ Start Context Resources	❏ Author Profile		
2	❏ Finish *To the Lighthouse* ❏ Continue Context resources	❏ Approach paper OR ❏ Retelling	❏ *Space Trilogy*	❏ Summary titles ❏ Approach paper
3	❏ Finish reading, watching, and listening to context resources.	❏ Write first draft of a 750-word essay 　❏ Use the rubric to check your paper 　❏ Proofread out loud 　❏ Turn it in for evaluation		
4	Additional reading ❏ Short stories	❏ Revise your draft based on the rubric and evaluation comments. ❏ Finish, proofread, and turn in your paper.		

Notes:
• You will find complete assignment instructions in the Assignment Schedule for this module.
• The suggested schedule may be adapted to fit your needs; just check off each assignment as you complete it.

Getting Started

"The main thing I try to do is write as clearly as I can. I rewrite a good deal to make it clear."
— E. B. White

Before you begin, set up a study area and English notebook to help you stay organized. If you learn how to do this now, you will be a step ahead when you get to college and realize that you are completely responsible for creating a time and place to learn. College professors usually hand out a syllabus at the first class, with all the assignments and due dates for the semester. They do not remind you of what is coming up, so if you do not have a method for keeping on top of everything, you can quickly fall behind. You will find the organizational techniques you learn from EIL helpful for any class you take in the future.

What belongs in a study area?

Study area basics are a comfortable chair, bright light, your English notebook and reading log, calendar or datebook, good dictionary, thesaurus, the EIL *Handbook for Writers* or other writer's handbook, pens, pencils, paper, sticky notes such as Post-it® notes, and possibly a computer. Being organized will make your study time more pleasant and productive, so be sure to start the school year by pulling together these things.

How to Use Items in Your Study Area

Chair and light: Read here (see the chapter on "How to Read a Book"). You want to be comfortable enough to enjoy the experience, but not so comfortable that you fall asleep. It is pleasant to read near a window, but you should also have a reading light positioned so that the light falls on your book. If you find that your eyes get tired quickly, you may need a brighter light or even reading glasses. Do not hesitate to get your eyes checked, so you can enjoy reading.

Calendar: Use a calendar or planner to record assignment deadlines, field trips, and other activities. At the beginning of each module, check the number of pages in your focus text and number of context resources; then plan how many you need to read daily in order to finish the focus text before you begin the essay.

English and Vocabulary notebook: Organize your English papers and vocabulary notes in a three-ring binder. The first page of your notebook should be an index page of the contents. You may make this as you add things, or use a copy of the Student Evaluation Summary in the back of this study guide as index starter. Next, put in a copy of each assignment you do, along with any mind-map or other note pages you'd like to keep and the evaluation rubrics you receive. Make a vocabulary section at the end of the binder (or tuck a small notebook into the pocket on the inside of the cover) with any new words and definitions you learn from each book. You may write these down in the order you discover them, or you may alphabetize them. The main thing is to remember them.

Commonplace book: Use a small blank notebook for copying beautiful or interesting passages from the books you read. I like notebooks with a dot grid as they help me keep my lines straight, but are less obtrusive than lines if I want to add a bit of calligraphy or copy a small sketch from the book. Choose what works for you. I keep a small Moleskine or Field Notes notebook in my purse and a larger (A5 or 5 x 8") Rhodia notebook in my planner so I can write down or read favorite quotes at any time.

Reading log: List everything you read—not just the books you read for English, but everything. Write the title, author, a one- or two-sentence summary of the book, and a comment and a rating. You may use the small *Reading Log* booklets I have on my web-store, EverydayEducation.com, or if you prefer to write lengthy reviews, you may prefer a blank journal.

Dictionary: Look up unfamiliar words you encounter. If you can guess their meaning from the context, just write down the word on a small sticky note and stick it on the page. Look it up after you are finished reading. If you cannot guess the meaning from the context, look it up before continuing. Looking up challenging words not only builds vocabulary and helps you remember the word, but also reveals the nuances in meaning that set the word apart from its synonyms. My favorite dictionary is the *Oxford Shorter English Dictionary* because most of the word usage examples are from literature. Many college dictionaries are acceptable as well.

Thesaurus: Use this when you find yourself repeating the same descriptive words over and over. I use *Roget A to Z*, which is organized alphabetically. The English language is fascinating, and there is a perfect word for almost any occasion—please find it and use it!

EIL *Handbook for Writers* or other handbook: Can't remember when to use a comma or a semicolon? Here is where you go to find out. Need instructions for how to write an expository essay? You will find it in your writer's handbook. A professional writer or editor always has several frequently used handbooks nearby. Writer's handbooks are packed with great information, and the reason professionals have several is that different handbooks have different areas of focus. No matter how competent you are as a writer, it is unlikely that you can remember every tiny detail of grammar, style, or usage, so it pays to check your handbook—chances are, you will find exactly the help you need.

Pens: Use a pen for mind mapping (thinking on paper) rough drafts, illustrations, Venn diagrams, and more. When I was in college, one of my favorite ways to study a long, challenging work was to use an 18" x 24" sketch pad and multi colored gel pens. I spent one semester in an in-depth independent study of Edmund Spenser's *The Fairie Queene* and found that the best way to see themes and remember what happened where was to summarize each book of the poem with a quick sketch (stick figures) and bullet points illustrating each canto.

Pencils: These are for writing in your books. Yes, I mean it—I want you to underline key passages, talk back to the characters, note thoughts that occur to you as you read, and so forth. This is called annotation, and it is part of active reading (you will learn more about this in the "How to Read a Book" chapter). Taking notes in the text will help you get the most out of a story. If you have to use library books for your focus texts, you will not be able to annotate as easily, but you can put a piece of paper in the back of the book and use it for the things you would normally write in the book.

Sticky notes: One of the first things to do is to make sticky-note tabs for your writer's handbook. This helps you turn quickly to key pages. For classes using an anthology, I recommend that at the beginning of the semester you look at the syllabus and go through the anthology and place a sticky-note tab with the author's last name and the title of the work beside each assigned piece. This saves time and helps remind you of what you have covered, and what remains.

Computer: When you reach college or the business world, you will need to know how to use a computer, so high school is the time to become comfortable with its basic functions. Rather than using a word-processing program on your computer, I suggest learning to use the free online word-processing program by Google. It is accessible through any Internet-connected computer, and your paper can be easily shared with a writing instructor, no matter where he or she is located.

Computer Tips

Formatting papers: Once you are in high school, all written work should be submitted in a college-style format. This means it should be typed in Times New Roman or a similar font, double-spaced, with one-inch margins all around (see the sample MLA paper in the back of this book). Be sure to have the grammar- and spell-check turned on in your word-processing program, but don't rely too heavily on these checking tools, because they are often wrong. Always do a "human proofread" by reading your paper aloud to yourself before turning it in. Reading aloud helps you slow down enough to spot typos and hear sentences or phrases that do not flow smoothly.

One space after terminal punctuation: Space only once after any terminal punctuation (period, question mark, etc.). Old typing instruction books used to require two spaces after terminal punctuation because typewriters use what is called a mono-spaced type, and the double spacing helped the eye distinguish the end of a sentence. Computer fonts are proportionally spaced, and proper spacing is programmed in. Double spacing creates unattractive blobs of white down a page and is a dead giveaway that outdated methods are being used.

Saving your document: Always create a computer folder for each class, and use a descriptive file name when you save your papers. For example, if you are writing the essay on Benjamin Franklin's *Autobiography* from the first module of *American Literature*, name the file "eil3-m1-franklin," and it will be easy to find anytime you need it.

If a paper gets "lost" on your computer: If you are new to the world of computers, you may occasionally think you have lost something on your computer. If you have been typing and your text seems to disappear, try pressing the Command key along with Z. This is the "undo" command, and it will undo the last thing you did, which should bring your paper back into view. If it does not, you can search your hard drive for the file name you used when you saved it. If you are using a Mac computer or Google Docs, any document should easily be found.

Frequently Asked Questions

Be curious always! For knowledge will not acquire you; you must acquire it.

—Sudie Back

If you have questions about any aspect of the curriculum or about studying in general, you may find the answers in this chapter.

Are all assignment instructions contained in this book?

This EIL guide contains the outline of the course, an assignment schedule for each module, models of the type of papers you will be writing, and evaluation information. In addition, you will need a copy of each of the novel-length focus works and a writer's handbook.

It is helpful to have old editions of Norton Anthologies of American, British, and World Literature for additional information and readings for each historical period. Beyond the basics, an atlas, art history book, and a dictionary of allusions are excellent optional additions to the study and reference tools listed here and in the "Getting Started" chapter.

You do not tell me how many pages to read each day. How will I know?

It is all about time management! This is a college-prep class, so you will be learning to look ahead and pace yourself. For modules based upon a novel-length work, you have a couple of options: 1) Sit down the first day and read the whole book in several hours; then use the rest of the time to gather supporting information; perhaps read another book by the author; and write your essay; or 2) Divide the book into two equal parts, and read one part per week, leaving the last two weeks to write and polish your essay. I prefer the first method, as the story is usually more interesting if it is not read in tiny fragments over a long period of time. This also leaves plenty of time to draft, revise, and polish your essay.

C. S. Lewis wrote that "a narrative style is not to be judged by snippets. You must read for at least half a day and read with your mind on the story" (from *English Literature in the Sixteenth Century Excluding Drama*). He is a wise guide, because immersion changes the experience of reading from an assignment to a journey into another world, another place, and another time. Whatever you do, start reading the first day of the module, and read every day until the book is finished. Do not procrastinate. And do not forget your context readings!

Can I use library books, or do I have to buy them?

I encourage active reading that includes annotation, especially of the focus works. This means underlining and making notes in the margin, and librarians really hate that. So I recommend you buy the focus books. You can probably find used copies fairly cheaply.

Is it better to own or to borrow books?

I have discovered that if you have books in your home, they will be read. I do not expect you to purchase all the resources I have referenced, but I hope you will consider having a few of the most important on hand. You can find them used at online retailers such as Amazon.com or Alibris.com, or you may even be able to get them free through PaperbackSwap.com (you may use my referral, "readbx"). I have purchased many books quite cheaply from library sales, thrift shops, and yard sales. Studies have shown that the number of books owned in a family has a direct relationship to the student's long-term academic success, with measurably higher test scores for book owners than for age mates with fewer books in the home.

Do you recommend a particular edition of each book?

It is important to have books that are pleasant to hold and read so that you enjoy the process and do not suffer from eyestrain. I do not recommend mass-market paperbacks, since they usually have too-small type, very small margins, and no scholarly introduction or discussion questions. Many are so hard to hold open that the spine is soon broken.

My favorite editions include Ignatius Critical Editions (best notes), Modern Library Paperback Classics. Norton, Penguin, and Oxford. The newest editions from these publishers are designed to lie open like a hardback, and they usually have insightful introductions and good discussion questions at the end. You will find links to each of my recommended editions at ExcellenceinLiterature.com.

Can I read the focus texts on an e-reader?

You can read the texts on an e-reader such as the Kindle® or Nook®, but it is not always easy to annotate as you are reading or to page back to look up a character or event. In addition, if you use free versions from the public domain, be aware that the available translations may not be of the best quality. If you decide to use an e-reader, be sure to learn how to highlight and add notes and bookmarks.

The assignment said to write a 500-word essay. I accidentally wrote 603 words. What shall I do?

You can edit to make your work tighter, which will usually make your paper better. As Strunk and White admonish in *Elements of Style*, it is best to "omit needless words." The second option is to not worry about it. The word count is a minimum rather than a maximum requirement. It is stated as number of words rather than number of pages so that teachers will not receive essays with 16-point type and 2" margins, because someone had to fill three pages and had no ideas. Word count allows no fudging.

What should go into the assignment header?

Every paper you turn in should have a proper heading as shown in the sample papers in the Formats and Models chapter. The heading should include your first and last name, the class name with the instructor's name on the same line, the date, and the essay prompt. The essay prompt is included to make it easy for the evaluator to determine whether your essay is on topic, and it is especially important for modules in which you have a choice of topics.

How do I download and print items from the Internet?

If you have done some Internet research, or if I have provided a link or URL to a resource you want to download and print, you can follow these steps:

1. If you have an ebook of EIL, you should be able to copy the URL from the text. Just copy (control + c) the entire URL, and paste (control + v) it into the address window of your browser, and click "enter."

2. If the page that appears offers a link to a printable copy, click the link to print directly from the screen.

3. If there is no link to a printable copy, hold down the left button of your mouse, and drag to select the text you want to copy.

4. Copy and paste the text into a blank TextEdit or Notepad file, and save it to your English folder or to a Google Drive or Evernote.com account online.

5. Go back to the web page where you found the information. Select the URL in the address line, and copy and paste it at the end of your text. Type in the date you accessed the website and any other information you think may be important. You may need some of this information for your Works Cited page.

6. Remember that it is never okay to copy material from anywhere and turn it in as your own work—this is called plagiarism, and it is a form of stealing. These suggestions are simply intended to help you if you need to save study resources you plan to quote in your essays or research paper.

Why are there a lot of Internet resources?

First, they are free and globally available. If you do not have a computer with Internet access, chances are that you can use one at your local library or at a friend's house. Second, you need to know how to use a computer responsibly, and how to find the kind of resources you will need for the future, whether that future involves college, business, or teaching your own children.

As you use EIL, you will encounter many useful sites and resources. You'll begin to see what is available online, and be able to recognize reliable sites for research. For several years, we have been adding good resources to our own Excellence-in-Literature.com website, so that's a great place to start your literary research.

What happens if a link does not work?

The context resource links are kept updated on the "Study Guide Links" pages at Excellence-in-Literature.com. If a link does not work for you, just type a few words of the title or author's name in the site search box at Excellence-in-Literature.com, and the resource should show up.

If you are typing in links and an EIL resource does not load, double-check each character you have typed and make sure it exactly matches the link provided. If you are using an e-book and you copy and paste the link, be sure not to pick up any punctuation near the link because that will keep it from working. If an online resource has been removed from its original site, we will have provided an appropriate alternative on the "Study Guide Links" pages.

Remember, if you don't find what you are looking for at the provided link, you can always do a search using keywords mentioned in the resource. For example, if you want to see more of the Mark Twain House and Museum, type "mark twain house museum" into your browser's search box, and you will find more resources and photos on that topic.

Do I have to read everything?

There are two things you absolutely must read, and they are this entire guide and each of the focus texts. I would like for you to read most of the context materials, but in a few cases there are more than you need. I have often included more than one suggested biography, simply because there are several good ones to choose from, and you may pick whichever one is easily available. The goal is for you to learn what you need to know in order to understand the author and the text and to write a thoughtful essay, not to just check off a random bunch of stuff.

I thought this was English class. Why do I have to look at art and listen to music?

Literature is a unique representation of its culture. Each great work was written by an author who was influenced by books, people, art, music, and events of his or her day. These influences, coupled with the author's education and family life, shaped the worldview that is inevitably reflected in their work.

In order to understand a poem, play, or story, it helps to understand a bit about the author and his or her philosophy of life. The biographical sketches can help with this, but sampling the art and music the author could have seen or heard is a different and sometimes more compelling way of gaining insight. The sights and sounds of an era can also help to illuminate the philosophy of life that shaped the focus text. You can think of content exploration as a virtual field trip!

How much time will EIL take each day?

The amount of time you spend depends on the length of the focus text and your reading speed. As an average, plan to spend at least one hour per day reading or writing about the focus text. Separate context reading or vocabulary work may add an additional 20–45 minutes per day.

Our family is different—do we have to follow the schedule exactly as it is written?

The schedule I have provided is the one my students followed when I taught these courses online (which I no longer do). It works efficiently and will help you enjoy all the books over the course of the school year. In addition, I arranged the modules to provide variation in type of reading and writing, and the modules graduate in difficulty from the beginning to the end of the year. However, I completely understand that each situation is unique. You may change the schedule, drop a module, take two years to cover the book, or alter it in any way that will help it better serve your family.

If you are teaching EIL in a co-op or school, you have the same liberty, though students who are following along in the book can probably be counted on to remind you that "That's not what Mrs. Campbell said to do!" Whatever you do, I promise that the EIL Enforcement Department will *not* stop by to rap your knuckles. The curriculum is here to serve you, and I want you to enjoy using it.

Why read old books?

There are many reasons to read old books, but author and apologist C. S. Lewis simply suggests that it is necessary in order to "keep the clean sea breeze of the centuries blowing through our minds" and to escape the "characteristic blindness of the twentieth century." He writes:

> It is a good rule, after reading a new book, never to allow yourself another new one till you have read an old one in between. If that is too much for you, you should at least read one old one to every three new ones.

> Every age has its own outlook. It is specially good at seeing certain truths and specially liable to make certain mistakes. We all, therefore, need the books that will correct the characteristic mistakes of our own period. And that means the old books. All contemporary writers share to some extent the contemporary outlook—even those, like myself, who seem most opposed to it . . . The only palliative is to keep the clean sea breeze of the centuries blowing through our minds, and this can be done only by reading old books . . . Two heads are better than one, not because either is infallible, but because they are unlikely to go wrong in the same direction.

(C. S. Lewis included these thoughts in his introduction to a translation of *Athanasius: On the Incarnation.* You may read more of the introduction by looking at the "Search Inside" feature for this book at Amazon.com.)

In an article on the Augustine College website, Professor Dominic Manganiello, D.Phil., concurs: "We will read old books, then, because in the past lie the foundations of our present and future hope. We will discover that the writings of the masters deal with 'primal and conventional things . . . the hunger for bread, the love of woman, the love of children, the desire for immortal life.'"

Finally, in perhaps the most compelling reason of all, Alexandr Solzhenitsyn pointed out that "literature conveys irrefutable condensed experience in yet another invaluable direction; namely, from generation to generation. Thus it becomes the living memory of the nation. Thus it preserves and kindles within itself the flame of her spent history, in a form which is safe from deformation and slander. In this way literature, together with language, protects the soul of the nation." You may read his entire 1970 Nobel Lecture at https://www.nobelprize.org/prizes/literature/1970/solzhenitsyn/lecture/.

How to Read a Book

If you don't have time to read, you don't have the time (or the tools) to write. Simple as that.

— Stephen King

No, you have not picked up the wrong course by mistake—this is indeed high school English! I know you have been reading for years, but I want to encourage you to learn to read deeply and thoughtfully. In this brief chapter I will review the way we approach excellent literature and give you tips on how to read well.

Reading is not about skimming over the words on a page. To read well is to enter in to the literature as into a work of art. In *An Experiment in Criticism*, C. S. Lewis suggests that we must "Look. Listen. Receive. Get yourself out of the way." He is right—we study great literature to learn and grow, not to impose contemporary ideas or criticisms upon it. As you read, you will encounter unfamiliar and possibly uncomfortable or unpleasant ideas, characters, or places. Instead of making a snap judgment about these things, consider why they are uncomfortable or unpleasant. What happens because of them, to them, or in them? This is the kind of immersion and contemplation that will help you grow as a reader and writer.

Reading Deeply

The difference between reading well and reading badly is like the difference between settling down to a leisurely and delicious steak dinner or gobbling a dry rice cake on the go. If you want to read well, you will neither rush nor gobble. A reader who reads well will close a finished book with traces of that book engraved in memory.

When you are ready to read, settle down in a quiet, comfortable spot with good light. Read without interruption, and seek to be a true reader, as C. S. Lewis describes it. He explains that "the true reader reads ... whole-heartedly [and] makes himself as receptive as he can" (*An Experiment in Criticism*). In addition, the true reader must, as Alexander Pope admonished, read "in the same spirit that the author writ." If you are reading something serious, take it seriously; if it's light, take it lightly.

Read Receptively

A work of . . . art can be either "received" or "used." When we "receive" it we exert our senses and imagination and various other powers according to a pattern invented by the artist.

C. S. Lewis

Reading good books can spark a variety of ideas and reflections. We aren't reading classics just to find out what happened, though that is part of it. We are reading them in order to enter into the experiences of another life; to discover what it is like to be entrusted with a quest or to live orphaned and alone. We read them to journey from burning Troy to Carthage and Italy with Aeneas or down the Mississippi River with Huck and Jim.

Books that have stood the test of time do so because they are such evocative portals into these other lives, times, and places. As you read, allow yourself to enter into the story with your imagination and all five senses. Smell the salt air of the wine-dark sea of Odysseus, and hear the creaking of oars and the splashing of waves. Imagine pangs of hunger and weakness so desperate that you are driven to ask a stranger for the porridge meant for a pig (*Jane Eyre*) or to steal a loaf of bread for which you spend years in a terrible prison (*Les Miserables*). To read is to enter in.

Reading Challenging Literature

Some books are meant to be tasted, some swallowed, and some few digested . . .

—Francis Bacon

The classics tell some of the most interesting, thought-provoking stories of all time. The challenge is that if you're haven't read many older books, they can seem difficult, or perhaps even dull because the storytelling style and pacing are difference from what we are accustomed to in the modern era. Readers in earlier centuries expected authors to create vividly detailed stories that allowed the reader to experience the story as if they were there, while many modern readers simply expect to breeze quickly through a book to find out what happened. As you've learned, breezing through is not what leads to reading well.

Here are a few suggestions to help you become more comfortable with older or more challenging books.

- **Immerse**: The key to enjoying any great book is to approach it first as a story. Read or listen all the way through, just as you would if you were reading *The Lord of the Rings* or any other book you enjoy.

- **Don't gobble**: Read all the way through, at a comfortable pace. Read fast enough to sustain interest, but slowly enough to understand what is happening. Seek to be immersed in the story; to see through the eyes of each character.

- **Use training wheels**: For the most challenging books, you may begin by reading a children's version or a brief synopsis of the work. This is not necessary for most works, but I have assigned it for those with archaic language, such as Chaucer's *Canterbury Tales* or for epic poetry such as Homer's *Odyssey*. Once you have read the synopsis or children's version of a difficult book, you will be ready to read or listen to the complete text.

- **Listen or watch**: If the assignment is poetry or a play, listen to it (even if you have to read it aloud to yourself in order to do so) or watch it as suggested in the assignments. Poetry is meant to be heard, and plays are meant to be seen and heard, so you must do this in order to fully appreciate them.

- **Gain insight**: Use the context resources to get acquainted with the history, art, music, poetry, and other literature relevant to the author or focus text. This helps you understand the author's artistic and cultural influences and can give you insight as to why the author wrote the story he/she wrote in the way that it is written.

- **Vocabulary**: As you read, keep an index card or piece of paper tucked into the back of the book, or write on the blank end pages. When you encounter words you do not know, do not interrupt the flow of the story as long as you understand the basic meaning from the context—just write down the word, look it up later, and add it to the list in your English notebook.

- **Annotate**: In your English notebook write down interesting insights that occur to you, as well as quotes that seem significant. Feel free to mark

Excellence in Literature: Reading and Writing through the Classics

important or interesting passages in the book (see the "Annotating" section later in this chapter) so that you can easily find them again while writing your essay.

- **Short writing assignments**: Once you have read the book, start the writing assignments. If you are working with a book not listed in this guide, write an approach paper according to the instructions in the Formats and Models chapter. The approach paper should include a brief summary, character analysis, discussion questions, key passage, and an explanation of the key passage. This will help you think through the book and prepare you for writing an essay.

- **Essay**: Write the assigned essay in response to the essay prompt. Believe it or not, writing thoughtfully about something specific in the book helps you gain insights you wouldn't otherwise have. Writing helps you learn!

Reading Fiction

If you are reading fiction, you will need to notice how the elements of **plot, theme, character, setting, and style** work together with **point of view** to create the alternate world of the story. However, as discussed in "Reading Deeply," it is also important to allow yourself to be immersed in the fictional world to the point that when you stop reading, you feel as if you have just returned from a long journey. Immersion makes it easier to see the story as a whole so that as you read you will recognize where you are in the plot. If the protagonist (the hero) is in terrible trouble, you're in the midst of conflict. If all the loose ends of

Freytag's Pyramid: The Shape of a Story

Did you know that the action in a plot can be visualized as a shape? German novelist Gustav Freytag created a diagram to show the form of a basic plot. Here is a simple example of Freytag's Pyramid, followed by brief definitions of each stage.

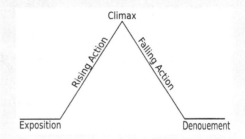

- Exposition: Here's where the scene is set, characters introduced, and the situation established. It usually falls at the beginning of the book, but additional exposition is often scattered throughout the work.

- Rising Action: Things get complicated in this section, with the conflict intensifying or even multiplying (think of a mystery in which more crimes are committed as detectives try to solve the first crime).

- Climax: The turning point in fiction; the transition from rising to falling action.

- Falling Action: Here's where the problems encountered during the rising action are solved.

- Denouement: Resolution or conclusion.

the story are being wrapped up, you've made it past the climax and are at the point of falling action, moving toward denouement.

If you are reading through the book with someone else, it can help to consider and discuss a few questions from the list at the end of this chapter. These are designed to help you move deeper into the text and prepare for the writing assignments. If the questions contain literary terms you don't know, look them up in the Glossary of this guide. If you need more information, consult your writer's handbook, check Excellence-in-Literature.com, or go to Google and type in "define:" (without the quotes) followed by the word or phrase you are looking for.

Reading Poetry

There is poetry in almost every module. Reading poetry is a bit different from reading prose (writing that is not poetry). Poetry uses structure, sound, and syntax to awaken the reader's imagination and to convey an image or message in a vivid and memorable way. A beautifully written poem can convey an idea in just a few unforgettable lines.

If you have not studied the analysis of poetry, it is especially important to review the process in one or more of the resources I have recommended. If you have the *Handbook for Writers* from EIL, you'll find a discussion of how to read and write about lyric poetry in Part 1: Section 10.8. Another resource you might find helpful is *Working it Out* by Joseph Womack. This little book offers a year-long study of the poetry of George Herbert, and in the process, demonstrates a simple and effective method for delving more deeply into any poem.

For now, here's how to begin understanding a poem. Start by reading it through slowly and carefully at least once or twice. Read it aloud, and listen to the sound of the words and pacing of the lines and syllables. Once you have the sound of the poem in your head, try paraphrasing it in prose. Think about each element and how the structure of the lines and the sound of the words contributes to the poem's theme. Examine the images, the rhyme scheme, and the sound patterns of the poem to help you understand the poet's message. Above all, read it through (or listen to it) in its entirety often enough that you see and remember it as a whole, just as you would look at a great painting as a whole before beginning to study the brush strokes.

Comedy and Tragedy

Although we sometimes think of comedy as something funny and tragedy as something sad, these words have a slightly different meaning in the study of literature. Comedy is a story that begins with a conflict or suffering and ends in joy, such as *Jane Eyre* or *A Midsummer Night's Dream*.

Tragedy is a story that begins at a high point and ends in pain, such as *Romeo and Juliet* or *Oedipus Rex*. In Veith's interesting chapter on comedy and tragedy, he suggests that the upward movement in comedy reflects a redemptive storyline, while the downward movement of tragedy reflects the archetypal fall of humanity. Aristotle further defined tragedy as the downfall of a noble human, in a disaster of his own making (*King Lear*).

Facing Challenging Ideas

Great literature tends to mirror life. A book becomes a classic because it creates an honest and true picture of life and accurately depicts the consequences of various philosophies of life. In portraying life accurately, complex and sometimes unpleasant issues arise, just as they do in life. Characters do or say things that are deeply wrong, as Macbeth did in giving way to ambition and committing murder, or less seriously, as Peter Rabbit did in stealing carrots from Mr. MacGregor's garden. However, each character experienced appropriate, true-to-life consequences for his actions, rather than an awkwardly contrived happy end. This is how literature can reflect life.

Gene Edward Veith specifically cautions conservative readers not to "seize upon a detail [such as a "bad word"] or a subject dealt with in a book, take it completely out of context, and fail to do the necessary labor of thinking about the work and interpreting it thematically" (72) before taking a stand against the book. He also cautions against stories that do not tell the truth about life. "Stories filled with 'good people' overcoming all odds may create the dangerous impression that human beings are, in fact, 'good' and capable of saving themselves through their own moral actions" (76). This type of plot is often found in genre fiction—what I call "Twinkies® for the brain"—and is what keeps these books from being great literature even when they tell an enjoyable story.

Annotating: Please Write in Your Books!

If you annotate your books as you read, you will understand and enjoy them more deeply than if you simply skim the text. Your annotations will also help you quickly locate important scenes in the book as you are doing the writing assignments for each module. Here are some suggestions for effective annotation.

- **Use a pencil** for writing in your books, as it does not show through and can be erased if necessary.

- Use the inside of the covers or the blank pages at the front and back for notes. Use an index card or piece of paper if you are using a library book.

- **Draw a vertical line** or star beside significant paragraphs.

- **Underline** important phrases or ideas.

- **Character List:** Use the inside of the front cover to list each of the characters in the order in which they appear. Include a brief note about the character's role in the plot or any distinguishing characteristics.

- **Timeline:** List each major event in the story as it happens. The inside back cover is a good place for this.

- **Sketch** small illustrations or write in subheadings (an especially fun and helpful thing to do for epic poetry (*Faerie Queene, Aeneid*, etc.)

- **Context:** If the focus text mentions a person, a piece of art, literature, or music, or a historic event, make a note in the margin and look up the item. Many of the poets, classical music compositions, and artistic works referenced in EIL can be found on the Excellence-in-Literature.com website.

- **Questions:** If you have a question about something in the text, write it in the margin. Writing it down will help you recognize the answer if it later appears in the text. If it does not appear, the written question will remind you to do a bit more research.

If You'd Like To Learn More

If you would like to delve deeper into the structure and analysis of literature, you'll find number of helpful resources in the "Selected Resources" chapter. Adam Andrews' brief *Teaching the Classics* DVD course introduces elements of literature and Socratic discussion using short stories. This course is brief enough to use over the summer before you begin EIL, or even concurrently.

If you are intrigued by the art of reading well, you may also want to read some of the essays on reading that I've mentioned in this chapter (Lewis, Pope, Aristotle) or *How to Read a Book,* Mortimer Adler and Charles Van Doren's classic guide to the art of reading. These resources and others are listed in the resources section at the end of this guide. Enjoy!

Questions to Consider as You Read

If you are not familiar with the terms used in this list, look them up in the Glossary at the back of the guide or in your writer's handbook. These questions may help you think through some of the stories or may be useful in a discussion, but you do not need to spend a lot of time with them.

- Who is the **narrator** of the story, and is he or she reliable or unreliable?

- What types of **conflict** do you see? Possibilities include man vs. man, man vs. God/fate/Providence/the gods, man vs. nature, man vs. society, or even man vs. himself.

- Should [character name] do [whatever he/she is planning]? Why/why not?

- What does it all mean? What great ideas (justice/mercy, friendship, good vs. evil, etc.) seem to be illustrated or embodied in the story?

- Who are the major and minor characters, and what kind of people are they? Consider physical, mental, moral, and spiritual dimensions.

- Do the challenges of the main character reflect common struggles of humanity? Is the character intended to portray an archetype?

- Can you identify the basic stages of the story structure—exposition (background information), rising action (complications), climax, falling action, resolution?

- How is the story told? Possibilities include first-person narrative, a journal, epistolary style (told as a series of letters), etc. How does this method affect your understanding of each of the story elements?

- Does the method of storytelling affect your enjoyment of the plot?

- What symbolism do you see, and how effectively does it enhance your understanding?

- Who or what is the antagonist—whoever or whatever is opposing the protagonist in the conflict?

- What role does each character play in revealing the story?

- What **plot devices** does the author use to move the story along? Possibilities include flashbacks, narrative frames, foreshadowing, genre-specific conventions, and so forth.

- Why has the author used a specific word rather than a synonym in the way and in the place he/she has used it? Would a synonym work as well? Why or why not?

How to Write an Essay

The time to begin writing an article is when you have finished it to your satisfaction.
By that time you begin to clearly and logically perceive what it is you really want to say.

—Mark Twain

An essay is a short writing assignment on a particular subject. According to the *Oxford Shorter English Dictionary*, the word *essay* is derived from the Latin root *exigere*, which means to ascertain or weigh. It is also defined as "a first tentative attempt at learning, composition, etc.; a first draft." The essay is sometimes called a position paper, because it must be an expression of the writer's conclusion about a matter, rather than a simple report.

Essays can be written to inform, explain, argue a position, or analyze an issue. Because the writer is expressing an opinion or interpretation, each essay can be seen as an attempt to persuade the reader that your thesis is plausible. Because the essay form involves all steps of the writing process, you will be able to apply the skills learned to any type of writing you do in the future.

In Excellence in Literature, you will have the opportunity to write essays, approach papers, literature summaries, author profiles, and various creative types of writing. The essay prompt in each module will provide an exact subject, and you will find that writing itself will turn into a process of discovery. You will rarely know the answer to the questions in the essay prompt until you begin writing, but as you consider what you have read, you can begin to formulate a thesis. From there, you will be able to write yourself into greater understanding and a reasonable conclusion.

The Writing Process

In the art of classical rhetoric, Cicero outlined five canons—stages or principles for structure or evaluation—for public discourse, especially oration or public speaking. We use three of these canons, Invention, Arrangement, and Style (the remaining two are Memory and Delivery) as guides for written composition. Here's what happens within each part of the process.

- Invention, also called Discovery, is the process of coming up with ideas;
- Arrangement, otherwise known as Disposition, is the process of organizing; placing ideas in the most logical and compelling order;
- Style, sometimes referred to as Elocution, is the process of appropriately and effectively expressing ideas.

This writing process provides a simple outline of what it takes to gather ideas, put them in order, and write them in a way that is understandable and appealing. The kinds of things you will do in each stage are listed and described below. Whatever you are writing—essay, research paper, story, song, poem, whatever—these are the basic things you will do to get yourself from a blank page to a completed project.

1. **Invention**
   - Read/Research
   - Think on Paper
2. **Arrangement**
   - Organize Ideas
3. **Style**
   - Write
   - Revise

Read and Research

To begin an essay assignment, gather information through reading and research. For Excellence in Literature assignments, this means you will read the focus text and assigned context resources, plus any other resources that seem relevant. If you look for additional research materials, be sure they are from reliable sources such as published encyclopedias and reference books, college websites, and original source documents.

Think on Paper with a Mind Map

When you "Think on Paper" in the second step of the writing process, you begin to connect your reading and research with the essay prompt. I use mind mapping to think on paper. This is a quick way to capture ideas and supporting points in an organic form that helps you think freely and creatively. Ideally, mind maps are written by hand, but this example was made with a free web app called Coggle.it.

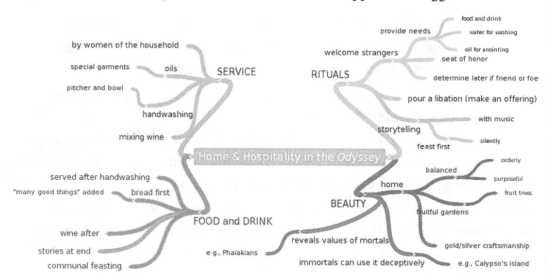

How to Make Your Own Mind Map

1. At the center of your paper, write a few words that summarize the topic or question you are supposed to answer.

2. Draw a line radiating from the center idea for each relevant fact, possible argument, proof point, or supporting detail that comes to mind.

3. Branch off these ideas as additional details emerge.

4. Write down everything that comes to mind, even if you are not sure it fits. Generating ideas is like turning on a faucet for hot water. What comes out at first is not hot, but it has to come out before what you really want can emerge. Your best ideas usually begin to flow after your mind has warmed up and settled into thinking about a topic.

5. Record each idea on the mind map as a word or phrase rather than a complete sentence, and feel free to use symbols and abbreviations to briefly capture your idea.

Additional Mind Mapping Ideas

- You may use color in your mind maps, but it is best not to create an elaborate color coding scheme before you start thinking on paper, as this can be distracting when you're trying to focus on ideas. I usually just add color during the organization stage.

- Some people prefer to use quick sketches rather than words to capture some or all of their ideas. If this is the way your mind works and it does not slow you down too much, feel free to draw.

- Mind maps are usually made with pen or pencil on paper, but you can also use small size sticky notes—one per idea—and make a mind map with those. Do what works for you.

- You can see many examples of mind maps at my Pinterest board for mind maps: pinterest.com/janicecampbell/mind-maps/.

Organize Ideas

Once you have generated several ideas, you must decide which ideas best fit the essay assignment, and how they might logically flow. Group ideas into three categories: Pro/Positive, Con/Negative, and Interesting. Once you have grouped your thoughts into these categories, you will probably have more ideas than you need. Select the most compelling points and interesting examples, and decide how to organize them.

Look at the ordered ideas, and determine whether your thesis will be a Pro/Positive or Con/Negative answer to the essay prompt, or whether you will take an equivocal position in which you provide evidence for and against both sides of the question and leave the reader to decide which perspective seems most compelling.

Thesis Statement

Draft a thesis statement that outlines your position and describes how you will support your argument. In its most elementary form, the thesis can be as simple as a transformation of the essay prompt into a thesis statement.

> **What is a thesis?**
>
> A statement or an opinion that is discussed in a logical way and presented with evidence in order to prove that it is true.
>
> *Oxford Learner's Dictionary*

On the next page, you'll find an example of what it looks like to turn a question—the essay prompt—into a thesis statement. The statement you will craft is similar to what you would write if you were told to answer a question in a complete sentence. It contains the essence of the question you are answering along with an indication of your answer and sometimes a pointer toward the reason for your example.

Question (adapted from a portion of the essay prompt in *American Literature* Module 2):

- How did the courtship strategies of Irving's characters compare to those of Longfellow's characters?

Question transformed into a thesis statement:

- Although Bram Bones and John Alden were successful in their respective courtships, their courtship strategies differed from one another in several specific ways, including [insert three ways here].

The thesis statement would usually appear near the end of the introductory paragraph, completing the job of orienting the reader to the topic and your position.

Topic Sentence Outline

It can be helpful to transform your list of ideas and supporting points into an essay framework by writing a topic sentence (TS) outline. You are not required to do this for every essay, but I recommend doing it for at least three of the modules in this book. It is simpler and more appropriate for the papers that you'll be writing than a classic alphanumeric outline, which works very well for longer pieces such as a research paper.

In this outline format, topic sentences introduce each supporting paragraph in the body of the essay and announce the proof you will be presenting in that paragraph. Following the topic sentence will be two or more sentences supporting the argument or providing the information found in the topic sentence. Here is an example of a topic sentence outline from the EIL *Handbook for Writers*, which provides detailed instructions for this type of outline:

Sample Outline For a Short Essay on Homer

General Subject: Homer's *Odyssey*

Focus 1: The importance of the home and hospitality

Focus 2: Home and hospitality in *The Odyssey*: the significance of food

Thesis: In *The Odyssey*, the frequent and detailed attention to food and the rituals surrounding it serve constantly to reinforce a central concern of the poem, the vital civilizing importance of the home.

TS 1: Throughout *The Odyssey*, we witness the way in which food taken communally can act as a way of re-energizing human beings, enabling them to cope with their distress. This, in fact, emerges as one of the most important human values in the poem. (Paragraph argues for the restorative values of food as brought out repeatedly in the poem.)

TS 2: The rituals surrounding food, especially the importance of welcoming guests to the feast and making sure everyone has enough, stress the warmth and central importance of open human interaction. (The paragraph argues the importance of hospitality as it is brought out by the references to food and feasting.)

TS 3: The occasions in which food is consumed are also moments in which the participants celebrate the artistic richness of their culture. No where else in the poem is there so much attention paid to the significance of beauty in various forms. (Paragraph X argues that all the things associated with the food—the serving dishes, the entertainment, and so on—reflect important values in the culture.)

Conclusion: There is, of course, much more to the poem than the description of feasting, but we need to recognize these moments as especially important. (Paragraph restates and summarizes the central point of the argument.)

Note: Remain flexible as you write, because it is quite possible to discover another angle or better idea as you are writing. If this happens, do not worry about sticking exactly to your outline. The outline is simply a tool for organization, so you, as the author, are still in charge. Do what works.

Write the Essay

Once you have organized your ideas, it is time to begin writing. At this stage, you have thoroughly thought through the question and your ideas, and have a sturdy framework to build on. Begin writing your first draft, following the general outline you have created.

Type your paper on the computer, following the formatting instructions contained in "Making Your Essay Look Good: The Basics of MLA Format," which is the last example in the **Formats and Models** chapter. At this stage, your primary concerns will be to successfully answer the essay prompt and to support your argument with relevant examples from the text. Look at the rubric in the back of the book to remind yourself of standards goals in the content, style, and mechanics of the paper.

Revise

When the draft is completed, read it aloud to yourself. This will help you pinpoint areas that seem unclear or poorly expressed. Do not skip this step! As you find things that need to be fixed, mark them and keep reading, so you do not lose the flow of the text. When you are finished, go through and fix the things you have marked. When it is as good as you can make it, turn it in.

When you receive the paper back from your writing mentor, read it aloud once again. You may be surprised to notice additional ways in which you can improve it. Refer to the evaluation rubric that you receive along with the essay, and make any improvements recommended there or in your teacher's marginal comments. Focus on fine tuning the style of the paper, including word choice, sentence fluency, and voice. You will find basic standards for these areas listed on the rubric, but your writer's handbook will help you learn even more.

Finally, when you have completed the edits recommended by your teacher, and you feel your essay meets the standards listed on the rubric, read it aloud once more. Change anything that does not sound right, check the mechanics, and when you are satisfied, turn it in.

As you follow this simple, orderly process in assignment after assignment, it will become automatic for you, and writing will become easier. By the time you reach college, you will be able to confidently tackle any writing assignment you encounter. I wish you joy in the craft of writing!

Resources You May Find Helpful

- *Excellence in Literature Handbook for Writers*
- *The Lost Tools of Writing* from the Circe Institute
- *The Elegant Essay Writing Lessons* by Lesha Myers
- *The Mind Map Book* by Tony Buzan
- *Writing to Learn* by William Zinsser

Discerning Worldview through
Literary Periods

*Every age has its own outlook. It is specially good at seeing certain truths
and specially liable to make certain mistakes. We all, therefore, need the books that will correct
the characteristic mistakes of our own period. And that means the old books.*

—C. S. Lewis

When you are studying literature in context, literary periods can help you understand a bit about the philosophy or worldview that undergirds the literary and artistic fashions of the day. You'll be able to see how the ideas of the Renaissance or the Modern periods are heard in the music of the time; seen in the arts; and embodied in the stories of the period. As you become acquainted with the assumptions that shaped each period, you can understand something about the author's influences before you even read the book.

There are six major periods or movements in English-language literature, and each is described below with its approximate time frame. Each period has sub-periods within it, as well as overlapping characteristics. I have chosen (with permission) to adapt and use the brief system of categories used by Adam Andrews in *Teaching the Classics*. These six major categories give you a very general overview of the period,; you will find greater detail at the <u>Excellence in Literature website</u>, with specific links referenced within the Context Resources. The six periods we will use are:

Medieval (AD 500–1500)

Renaissance (1500–1660)

Neoclassical (1660–1800)

Romantic (1800–1865)

Realist (1840–1914)

Modernist (1900–1945)

Medieval (AD 500–1500)

The **Medieval** period includes the Anglo-Saxon period in the time before the 1066 Norman conquest of England, and the Middle English period after the conquest. **Anglo-Saxon** literature, which is based on oral storytelling, focuses on the heroic ideal which involved responsibility, leadership, loyalty, generosity, and skill in battle. After Christianity reached Britain in the seventh century, literature became overwhelmingly Christian in its themes, while still retaining its concern for the heroic ideal. The epic poem *Beowulf* is a characteristic work from this period.

The **Middle English** period was marked by a change in the purpose and audience for written literature. Anglo-Saxon works had been written by and for the aristocracy, but Middle English literature was by and for people of the lower classes. Rather than the idealized king-heroes of the Anglo-Saxon period, Middle English heroes were everyday people living in everyday situations. Christianity remained central to the medieval world, and most literature reflected this priority. This literary movement roughly coincided with the Gothic period in art and architecture. A well-known work of this period is *The Canterbury Tales* by Geoffrey Chaucer.

Renaissance (1500–1660)

The Renaissance period was a flamboyant, fervent era of exploration and expansion, characterized by several movements, including Renaissance humanism, the Protestant Reformation, Catholic Reformation, and English Nationalism. Renaissance writers were concerned with classical learning, the study of the humanities (language, literature, history, art, and government), the function of religion in the world, and interest in the form and structure of human government. This literary movement roughly coincided with the baroque period in art, music, and architecture.

Authors you will recognize from this period include William Shakespeare, Edmund Spenser, John Donne, and Anne Bradstreet.

Neoclassical (1660–1800)

The Neoclassical period in literature, art, and music roughly coincided with the Age of Enlightenment. Writers in the Neoclassical period favored simplicity, clarity, restraint, regularity, and good sense, as opposed to the intricacy and boldness of the Renaissance period. Neoclassical writers sought to discover meaning in the order of things, placed society before the individual, and viewing humanity as inherently flawed, valued human reason over natural passions. Many of these writers were influenced by the rise of experimental science and the desire for peace and stability. Many sought to imitate the style of Roman writers such as Virgil and Ovid. The art, architecture, and music of this period reflected the aesthetic values of this literary movement.

Writers of this period include Benjamin Franklin, Daniel Defoe, and Jonathan Swift.

Romantic (1800–1865)

Following the French Revolution there was general movement away from the formal literature of the Neoclassical period. Romantic art, music, and literature reflected a belief in mankind's innate goodness, equality, and potential for achievement, and strongly rejected the Neoclassical view of man as a limited being in a strictly hierarchical society. Possibly as a reaction against urbanization and other challenges of the Industrial Revolution, nature was prominently featured as a symbol of freedom of the human soul, and scenic beauty as a model for harmony. Emotion, imagination, and intuition were valued above reason and restraint. This period includes Early and Mid-Victorian literature.

Authors in this tradition include Sir Walter Scott, Mary Shelley, James Fenimore Cooper, and Johann Wolfgang von Goethe.

Realist (1840–1914)

Just as Romantic writers had rejected Neoclassical ideas, Realist authors, artists, and musicians rejected Romantic notions. Realists sought to portray the world and man without idealism, so their works dealt with issues such as industrialization, poverty, and inequality, sometimes focusing on the ugly or sordid. They were interested in the relationship between traditional religion, rationalist thought, and new philosophies such as Darwinism. In England, the Realist period takes place largely during the reign of Queen Victoria (1837–1901), so it includes Mid- and Late Victorian literature.

Realist writers you may know include Charles Dickens, Willa Cather, the Brontë sisters, Booker T. Washington, and Mark Twain.

One form of realism that lasted until World War II was known as **Naturalism**. Influenced by Charles Darwin's theory of evolution, Naturalist writers believed that social conditions, heredity, and environment, rather than Providence or Fate, determined man's destiny, and they often wrote about those on the fringe of society, including the uncouth and sordid. If Romantics saw the individual as a god and Realists saw him as a common man, Naturalists saw him as a helpless animal for whom free will was only an illusion. Naturalist writers include Jack London and Stephen Crane.

Modernist (1900–1945)

The dramatic changes wrought by the Industrial Revolution, Marxism, and modern scientific theories and political developments rocked the faith of twentieth-century writers. At the heart of Modernist literature is a reflection of their conviction that all the traditional structures of human life—religious, social, political, economic, and artistic—had either been destroyed or proven false. The writers' disorientation and uncertainty is often seen in the fragmented form of their fiction, and their protagonists are often aimless and frustrated rather than heroic.

Modernist authors include F. Scott Fitzgerald, Gertrude Stein, T. S. Eliot, Ernest Hemingway, and Ezra Pound.

After World War II, the Modernist movement split into fragments such as Post-Modernism, Imagism, the Harlem Renaissance, Surrealism, Beat poets, Post-colonialists, and others. It is not clear which, if any, of these will prove dominant in historic hindsight. What is certain is that each of the literary periods explored here will help you understand the literature you read, in the context in which it was created.

This summary of literary periods is adapted from Teaching the Classics, *and is used courtesy of Adam Andrews, www.CenterForLit.com.*

If you'd like to know more about worldview, please see the "What is a Worldview?" explanation by Dr. Kenneth H. Funk II, available from the Excellence-in-Literature.com website.

Tips for Using EIL in a Classroom

Words are a lens to focus one's mind.

-Ayn Rand

Teachers are using this curriculum in so many creative ways in classrooms and co-ops everywhere. Eventually, I hope to establish a spot on Excellence-in-Literature.com or our Facebook page for teachers to exchange ideas and find support, but until then, here are few suggestions for using EIL with a group.

First, remember that one of the key features of EIL is the practice of college-level learning skills in addition to literary analysis. C. S. Lewis writes that "Ideally, we should like to define a good book as one which 'permits, invites, or compels' good reading. but we shall have to make do with 'permits and invites'" (*An Experiment in Criticism*, 113). The books in EIL are the kind that permit and invite good reading to those with a receptive ear. Good literary discussions can encourage deeper reading and more thoughtful written responses, so they can be a great benefit even if the discussion takes place in a very small group.

To encourage participation, students should prepare for discussions by doing all the assigned readings before class time. For small groups, each student can be assigned to make a short presentation on a chapter, a portion of the context resources, or on a specific discussion question. The teacher or co-op leader should function as a facilitator, assigning areas of research and guiding discussions, rather than doing the research and lecturing on findings.

As Charlotte Mason admonished, "We err when we allow our admirable teaching to intervene between children and the knowledge their minds demand. The desire for knowledge (curiosity) is the chief agent in education: but this desire may be made powerless like an unused limb" (*A Philosophy of Education*, p. 247). She asks, "What if the devitalisation we notice in so many of our young people, keen about games but dead to things of the mind, is due to the processes carried on in our schools, to our plausible and pleasant ways of picturing, eliciting, demonstrating, illustrating, summarising, doing all those things for children which they are born with the potency to do for themselves?" (p. 237). Simply stated, learning happens when students interact with literature, not when they listen passively to a lecture.

Here are a few ideas for creating an active group learning environment:

- Introduce each module by pointing the student to the Module Focus, Literary Context, and Introduction in the text.

- Assign a context area to each student or group of students, and have them report their findings to the class.

- If the Focus Text is a poem, encourage students to listen to at least a portion of it in a professionally recorded audio version. A poem is meant to be heard, and listening will bring it to life as nothing else can.

- For each module, have students choose one passage or poem to recite or copy by hand. Recitation and copywork both aid retention of ideas and build writing skills, as both require close attention to the use of words and sequence of ideas.

- If the Focus Text is a play, always try to watch the video version. It may be best to watch it after the focus text has been read, so students will be able to appreciate subtle twists and nuances they may otherwise miss.

- Use the *Something to Think About* and *Be Sure to Notice* items as discussion starters after students have begun reading the text.

- Pull a few of the "Questions to Consider as you Read" for discussions. The most fruitful questions tend to be those that evoke an opinionated response:

  - Should [character name] do [whatever he/she is planning]? Why or why not?

  - What does it all mean? What great ideas (justice/mercy, friendship, good vs. evil, etc.) seem to be illustrated or embodied in the story?

- What can you learn, or what do you think the author believes you should do or not do?

- Encourage additional research or sharing of context items not found in the EIL guide. If students find a resource they particularly like, they are welcome to submit it to me at Janice@EverydayEducation.com for possible inclusion in the next edition of EIL.

- When students do an approach paper, choose some of their discussion questions to spark discussions in class. If students have chosen different key passages (this is perfectly fine), encourage them to discuss why they chose the passage they did, and why it is a key.

- When students have finished the focus text, encourage discussion of how it exemplifies its literary period, and ways it may have differed from student expectations.

- If you choose to watch the movie version of a novel as part of the class, discuss how it differs from the author's creation.

- Encourage comparison of the current focus text with other works the student has read in or out of class. As they learn to discern common themes, you may find them referencing *Les Misérables*, *Merchant of Venice*, *The Little Red Hen*, and *The Lion, the Witch and the Wardrobe* in discussions of justice and mercy, love and duty. This means they are seeing *through* each story into the broader story beyond, which is a sign that they are reading deeply and well.

- If you have five classroom periods each week, use one to practice what my high school used to call USSR—Uninterrupted, Sustained, Silent Reading. Many students have never been required to sit quietly for an hour and do anything, but this is an essential skill that needs to be learned, and USSR is a good way to begin. (For more on brain development and the effect of technology on language skills, I recommend *Endangered Minds* and *Failure to Connect* by Dr. Jane Healy.)

Comprehension Questions

I do not believe in using "comprehension questions" at all, except in a very limited way as practice for necessary standardized testing. I do not believe they are useful or effective, especially for high school students who should be learning to love literature, think deeply, and write thoughtfully about the literature they read.

Comprehension questions are often trivia questions which test only student memory or the ability to catch details. Instead of helping students think deeply about the text as a whole, comprehension questions often make reading nothing more than a treasure hunt for answers. I have seen "how to study" guides that suggest students should read the comprehension questions first, then hunt for answers as they skim the story. This may be an effective strategy for timed standardized tests and may seem to be a quick and easy way to finish an assignment and move on, but it completely short circuits the learning process. Plus, it is a fast way to ruin a great book.

The writing prompts provided in EIL encourage students to thoughtfully and analytically consider something specific about the text. It is impossible to write a coherent, thoughtful paper without comprehending what you have read, so it provides a much better measure of how much the student understands about the literary work, and how well he or she writes.

Module 4.1

Beowulf

> *Often, for undaunted courage, fate spares the man it has not already marked.*
>
> —Lines 572-573

Focus Text

Beowulf: A New Verse Translation by Seamus Heaney or J. R. R. Tolkien

Honors Texts

The Dream of the Rood

Caedmon's Hymn or *The Battle of Maldon*

Good translations of both these poems are included in *The First Poems in English*, a Penguin Classics anthology linked from the Excellence in Literature.com website. They are also widely available online, but the quality of translations vary.

Literary Period

Medieval: Anglo-Saxon

Module Focus

We will look at the conventions of epic poetry and the concept of the heroic ideal in medieval literature.

Introduction

Beowulf has endured through the ages, not because it is a stuffy example of Anglo-Saxon epic poetry, but because it is a rollicking good tale of heroism with super-heroes, battles, monsters, and a dragon. There is much to enjoy in *Beowulf*, and Seamus Heaney's poetic translation from the Old English brings the story to life. Be sure to listen to it as well as read it, so that you can fully appreciate the artistry of the writer and the translator.

Something to think about . . .

J. R. R. Tolkien, author of *The Lord of the Rings* and *The Hobbit* and other works, was a professor of medieval literature. One of the works he studied was *Beowulf*, and he even wrote a prose translation of it. If you are familiar with *The Lord of the Rings*, you will be able to see how Tolkien's knowledge of Old English, the medieval era, and the conventions of the epic helped to shape the story of Middle Earth. If you have not read Tolkien's books, I highly recommend them.

Be sure to notice . . .

Epic Characteristics

- Long narrative poem (tells a story)
- Vast setting
- Develops episodes important to history of a nation, state, people
- Didactic, giving lessons on appropriate action for the audience
- Great deeds by a hero of mythical, legendary, or historical significance; a person of heroic proportions, high position
- Supernatural forces intervene
- Elevated style, reflected in formal speeches by main characters

Epic Conventions

- Poet states theme at opening
- Invokes muse
- Begins *in medias res*—exposition comes later
- Catalogues of warriors, ships, armies, weapons
- Extended formal speeches
- Frequent use of epic similes—formal and sustained; an epic simile is an extended comparison using figurative language

Context Resources

Readings

If you are a little intimidated at the thought of tackling medieval poetry, you may want to read through this very useful *Beowulf for Beginners* site, complete with entertaining illustrations.

https://www.abdn.ac.uk/sll/disciplines/english/beowulf/

If your version of the poem does not have the Old English original, you may want to view a hypertext version with helpful annotations and other good information.

https://www.humanities.mcmaster.ca/~beowulf/

If your library has the prose translation by J. R. R. Tolkien, it is well worth reading. Read a bit more about the Tolkien translation:

https://www.newyorker.com/magazine/2014/06/02/slaying-monsters

Tolkien also wrote a significant essay, "Beowulf: The Monsters and the Critics," which can be helpful in understanding the ideas that shaped the story.

https://notendur.hi.is/peturk/KENNSLA/OE/TEXTS/Tolkien_Monsters.pdf

What values motivated Beowulf? This brief article will introduce you to what the Anglo-Saxon world honored.

https://www.researchgate.net/publication/333675201_Anglo-Saxon_values_and_culture_in_Beowulf

Professor Sara Selby's brief history of the English language may help you understand the story behind the Anglo-Saxon language of *Beowulf*:

https://excellence-in-literature.com/a-micro-history-of-the-english-language/

The British Library, which holds the first known *Beowulf* manuscript, has an excellent site on how language changes. It explores the development of English from the earliest Anglo-Saxon to contemporary prose. To gain a better understanding of *Beowulf* and its context, I recommend reading the *Changing Language* homepage, the Language Timeline, Language and the Written Word, and the *Beowulf* related Activities.

https://www.bl.uk/medieval-literature

The Seamus Heaney translation has a good family tree in the back of the book, but you will need to keep track of minor characters as well. I suggest printing out the character list at the site below.

http://csis.pace.edu/grendel/proj1b/names.html

The Author's Life

Because this poem is so very old, we know nothing concrete of the author. You may read of the poem's fascinating history in this essay by Robert F. Yeager.

https://excellence-in-literature.com/why-read-beowulf-by-robert-f-yeager/

Poetry

Cædmon is known as the first English poet, so don't miss this brief legend of how he became a poet.

https://imagejournal.org/article/caedmons-hymn-the-first-english-poet/

At *The Complete Corpus of Anglo-Saxon Poetry*, you will find links to many interesting poems, riddles, and prose pieces, including translations of Genesis, Exodus, and Daniel. Read at least three things, and consider how they are similar to or different from Beowulf.

https://www.sacred-texts.com/neu/ascp/

Audio

In order to appreciate the poem, you need to hear it. You can hear recordings of significant passages read by Seamus Heaney at the Beowulf Resources site. Don't miss this!

https://www.beowulfresources.com/
hear-seamus-heaney-read-his-translation-of-beowulf/

An alternative is the Audible recording by Julian Glover.

https://amzn.to/3aRiMFG

Librivox has an amateur reading of the entire poem, but I do not recommend it unless you cannot find a more professional recording (check your library or Audible.com).

https://librivox.org/beowulf-by-unknown/

Music

Musician Benjamin Bagby performs a stunning bard version of *Beowulf*, using the Anglo-Saxon harp and his dramatically resonant voice. Listen to an interview with him at the first link, and read more about him and listen to a video clip of the *Beowulf* performance at the second. Is this how you imagined a bard might sound?

https://www.wnyc.org/story/46300-ear-to-ear-benjamin-bagby/

http://www.bagbybeowulf.com/video/index.html

https://amzn.to/3dK4oTo

Regia Anglorum offers a nicely illustrated overview of the music and instruments of the Anglo-Saxon era.

https://regia.org/research/misc/music.htm

If you would like to listen to medieval music such as plainchant or Renaissance polyphony as you study, check your local library or a streaming service for Gregorian chant or music by Palestrina, Thomas Tallis, or William Byrd.

You can hear samples of the *Beowulf* movie soundtrack at Amazon.com. It is a very modern interpretation, so do not expect a medieval sound.

https://amzn.to/2NtDHFW

Video

There are several movie versions of *Beowulf*, but I have not seen any of them, so I cannot make a recommendation. You may view some clips and reviews that will help you decide if you are interested in seeing one.

http://www.imdb.com/find?s=tt&q=beowulf

Here is another, more exciting *Beowulf* battle scene clip from Benjamin Bagby's performance:

https://excellence-in-literature.com/beowulf-battle-scene-benjamin-bagby

Visual Arts

View a map of the land of the Geats and Danes, with Beowulf's voyage marked.

https://www.abdn.ac.uk/sll/disciplines/english/beowulf/voyage.htm

The Electronic Beowulf project website has digitized and annotated pages of an early handwritten *Beowulf* manuscript. The accompanying article is about what it takes to digitize and preserve these ancient manuscripts, so you don't have to read it unless you're interested. Just look at the different pages of the poem, and imagine a time in which all books had to be written by hand. If all the books in the world were going to disappear and you could only keep what you copied for yourself, what books would you choose to copy?

http://www.uky.edu/~kiernan/welcome/1993.htm

Pictorial Guide to Beowulf offers maps, photos of weapons and armor, and much more. Look at all that interests you, and do not miss the beautiful image of the reconstructed mead hall. Clicking on images will enlarge them.

https://heorot.dk/beo-guide.html

If you have an art history book or can get one from your local library, look at the section on medieval art. This will give you some insight into what the people of the Middle Ages found important, and you will see the kind of armor, ships, and castles that are mentioned in *Beowulf.*

Take a look at the illustrations from various editions of *Beowulf* at the "Beowulf on Steorarume" (Beowulf in Cyberspace) site. Which of these vivid interpretations of the story do you prefer?

https://heorot.dk/beowulf_art/

If you do not have an art history book, *Medieval Art and Architecture* is an interesting site with links to many medieval images. View at least a few links, so that you will have a clear vision of medieval priorities.

http://www.medart.pitt.edu

Historic Context

Here's a brief overview of Anglo-Saxon history. Be sure to notice where they came from and where they settled.

https://www.bl.uk/anglo-saxons/articles/who-were-the-anglo-saxons

Assignment Schedule

Week 1

Begin reading the context resources and the poem. As you read the poem, you will find compound descriptions, called "kennings," that are often used in Anglo-Saxon poetry. Examples include "frothing wave-vat" for ocean, world-candle, bloody-toothed slayer, hoard-guard, and more. Copy each kenning you find, along with your interpretation of what it describes. If you enjoy kennings, you may like the extra definition and activity at the following link:

http://mseffie.com/assignments/beowulf/kennings.html

Week 2

When you finish the poem, write a historical approach paper on Anglo-Saxon England. You will find the format and a sample paper in the Formats and Models chapter. In addition to the context links I have provided, you may use other resources such as your encyclopedia, the library, and quality Internet resources to complete this assignment. Be sure to refer to your writer's handbook if you have questions about grammar, structure, or style.

Week 3

Begin drafting a 750-word paper on one of the topics below. I recommend that you follow the writing process outlined in the "How to Write an Essay" chapter, consulting the models in the Formats and Models chapter and your writer's handbook as needed.

1- Model: *Beowulf* and the MLA Format Model

Prompt: Retell *Beowulf* with a modern setting and characters, retaining the balanced tone and pacing of the original version. Remember that this is a classic story of good and evil, and in modern times an enemy may be vanquished by means other than death. Your story should be at least 750 words and may be as long as necessary to tell a good tale.

2- Model: Literary Analysis Essay and MLA Format Model

Prompt: In *Beowulf*, you will find a blend of medieval Christian and pagan beliefs, with the pagan belief in Wyrd or Fate coexisting with a Christian belief in a savior-God known as the Word. The poem praises heroic virtues such as courage, loyalty, and the willingness of a hero to die for his people. Beowulf embodies virtues from both Christian and pagan cultures. Draft a 750-word paper considering ways in which the virtues from each culture similar or different. Be sure to use quotes from the text to support your thesis.

Turn in the draft at the end of the week, so your writing mentor can evaluate it using the Content standards (Ideas/Concepts and Organization) on the rubric.

Week 4

Use the feedback on the rubric along with the writing mentor's comments to revise your paper. Before turning in the final draft, be sure you have addressed any issues marked on the evaluation rubric, and verify that the thesis is clear and your essay is well-organized. Use your writer's handbook to check grammar or punctuation so that your essay will be free from mechanical errors. Turn in the essay at the end of the week so that the writing mentor can use the evaluation rubric in the "How to Evaluate" chapter to check your work.

Module 4.2

Canterbury Tales by Chaucer (1343–1400)

This noble ensample to his shepe he yaf,—
That first he wrought, and afterwards he taught.

—*Canterbury Tales*. Prologue. Line 498

Focus Text

Canterbury Tales by Chaucer

Use a good annotated translation (Modern Library Classics, Norton, or Oxford), or this module will be very challenging. Read the following portions:[1]

- Prologue
- The Knight's Prologue and Tale
- The Squire's Prologue and Tale
- The Pardoner's Prologue and Tale (also known as the Pardon-Peddlar's Tale)
- Sir Thopas' Prologue and Tale
- The Tale of Melibee
- The Monk's Prologue and Tale
- The Nun's Priest's Prologue and Tale
- The Canon's Yeoman's Prologue and Tale (also known as the Cleric-Magician's Servant's Tale)

[1] If you choose to read the entire text, please be aware that medieval humor in a few of the stories can be crude, and some translations are worse than others.

- Here the Maker of This Book Takes His Leave

Librarius offers a good side-by-side version of the book, with a Middle English glossary. This is a supplement only—you need to read it in a book so that you can write in the text.

http://www.librarius.com/cantales.htm

Honors Text

Piers Plowman by William Langland

Literary Period

Medieval: Middle-English

Module Focus

We'll consider the use of a framed narrative and its effect on the story and become familiar with Middle English.

Introduction

Canterbury Tales is one of the greatest works of medieval fiction and a superb example of a framed narrative. Author Geoffrey Chaucer gathered a motley crew of fictional characters, each with a different story to tell, and framed the collected narratives in a story of his own. Chaucer uses both the stories and the character's physical appearance to reveal each individual's personality and character traits. You will see admirable people and scoundrels, humor and hypocrisy, throughout the tales as well as in the narrative frame. Enjoy!

Something to think about . . .

Like many writers of the medieval era, Chaucer wrote primarily in poetry rather than prose. Why do you think that might be?

Be sure to notice . . .

Canterbury Tales is a "framed narrative," or a story within a story. Chaucer has used the story of pilgrims telling stories on a long journey to pull together the various tales and give them a literary "frame." In an interesting and unusual move, he places himself into the story as the frame's narrator. Does this make the story seem more or less believable?

Context Resources

Readings

The Canterbury Tales, retold by Geraldine McCaughrean, is a good retelling of the tales in prose. This is an illustrated version for middle-grade readers, but if you read it or any brief modern-language version before starting the Middle English version, you will be better prepared to understand each story.

https://amzn.to/3bFoSoq

Read portions of "The General Prologue," "The Pardoner's Prologue and Tale," and "The Nun's Priest's Tale" in the original Middle English. If you are having a hard time comprehending Chaucer's language, try reading it aloud. When pronounced phonetically, many of the words sound very similar to things we would find in the King James Version of the Bible, and it is almost easier to hear the meaning of the stories than it is to read them.

You can "Teach Yourself to Read Chaucer's Middle English" by following the tutorial on this page. This is nicely done and will help you as you work with the Middle English text.

https://chaucer.fas.harvard.edu

Gode Cookery presents *The Life and Times of the Canterbury Tales Pilgrims*, a delightful site that provides a wealth of interesting detail about the personal lives of the pilgrims. This is well worth exploring.

http://www.godecookery.com/pilgrims/pilgrims.htm

Sometimes a contemporary book offers an alternative way to get acquainted with an ancient work such as Chaucer's. The "history mystery" *Who Murdered Chaucer?* by Terry Jones, et al., is an interesting introduction to the turbulent fourteenth century. You may read reviews at Amazon.com to determine if this is a resource you might enjoy.

https://amzn.to/3uwTXGz

The University of York offers *Pilgrims and Pilgrimage*, a detailed look at the concept and purpose of the pilgrimage, particularly in the Christian culture. This will help you understand the purpose of the pilgrims' journey.

https://www.york.ac.uk/projects/pilgrimage/

The pilgrims were journeying toward Canterbury Cathedral. How well did they embody the classical virtues as they made their journey? This printable poster of the virtues will help you remember them as you read.

http://www.keithbuhler.com/virtues (PDF)

The Author's Life

In the *Norton Anthology of English Literature* (or in the introduction of another good, annotated version of the story), read the mini-biography of Chaucer and the overview of *The Canterbury Tales*.

Harvard University offers an excellent Chaucer site with a good timeline of Chaucer's life, and links to details about events such as the Black Death, Chaucer's capture by the French, and his royal service. I highly recommend reading through this.

https://chaucer.fas.harvard.edu

The Luminarium, created and maintained by Anniina Jokinen, offers excellent information about Chaucer, with a long biography, many links, and lots of good contextual information. Luminarium is run by an individual, but the material seems well-researched and highly respected. For more info on the author, see "A Letter from the Editor":

http://www.luminarium.org/letter.htm

http://www.luminarium.org/medlit/chaucer.htm

The BBC offers a very brief introduction, plus a few additional insights on Chaucer's life and works. He is an interesting character!

https://www.ancient.eu/Geoffrey_Chaucer/

Poetry

The Italian poet Dante Alighieri is thought to have influenced Chaucer in his work. This Harvard site offers a few quotations that will help you see the connection.

http://www.courses.fas.harvard.edu/~chaucer/special/authors/dante/

Audio

Be sure to listen to at least part of *The Canterbury Tales* in audio format. They are very interesting that way, as a good narrator can bring the different characters to life and make them much more memorable. Check for a good version of the Tales at your library or on a streaming service.

http://librivox.org/the-canterbury-tales-by-geoffrey-chaucer/

Chaucer didn't compose his poem in modern English and we have no recordings of what the language sounded like when the Tales were composed. Here is a short recording of an English professor reading Chaucer the way scholars think it was probably pronounced. It is very entertaining and a great way to get the "sound" of Chaucer in your ear.

https://alanbaragona.wordpress.com/the-criyng-and-the-soun/

Here is another professor's version of the Prologue. Nicely done.

http://pages.towson.edu/duncan/chaucer/index.htm

Finally, here is a simple PDF guide to the different between Old, Middle, Early Modern, and Late Modern English. Be sure to read the short explanations of the differences.

https://web.cn.edu/kwheeler/documents/OE_vs_ME.pdf

Music

Professor Alan Baragona at Virginia Military Institute (VMI) has gathered clips of fourteenth-century music. These are the type of sounds Chaucer and his contemporaries may have heard in both formal and informal settings.

You may listen to beautiful choral pieces by Thomas Tallis here:

https://excellence-in-literature.com/thomas-tallis-medieval-music/

Video

An animated version of *The Canterbury Tales* was filmed in 1998 and won an award for the Best Animated Short Film. It is most easily available in England, but your local library or college library may have a copy.

Visual Arts

The Visualizing Chaucer Library Project has gathered illustrations from many versions of *The Canterbury Tales*. Notice how the illustration styles change through different artistic periods.

https://d.lib.rochester.edu/chaucer

The pilgrims were on their way to the Canterbury cathedral. You can see a number of good photos with detailed contextual information at Jane Zatta's scholarly website.

http://englishcomplit.unc.edu/chaucer/zatta/canterbury.htm

At Mulder Media you will find a nicely presented gallery of illuminated manuscripts. They are shown as pages in a book, and the "back" and "next" buttons move you through the text. There are also links to other manuscript sites on the web.

http://www.muldermedia.com/gallery/index.html

If you are interested in learning about the various historical editions of Chaucer's *Canterbury Tales*, you can view some fascinating images and find out more about the various surviving manuscripts at this interesting website from the University of Wisconsin:

https://chauceratwisc.wordpress.com/manuscript/

Look at fourteenth-century artists in an art history book, paying special attention to Giotto di Bondoni (c. 1267 - 1337), an artist whose work influenced Chaucer. You may also view his work and read a brief biography online.

https://www.giottodibondone.org

http://www.ibiblio.org/wm/paint/auth/giotto/

Stained glass was another major art form in the medieval period. Scroll down on this page to see a few stunning examples (you may need to use Internet Explorer in order to see them—other browsers may not work as well).

https://www.metmuseum.org/toah/hd/glas/hd_glas.htm

The Victoria and Albert Museum offers a virtual tour of a Gothic art exhibition that will help to round out your picture of what this era looked like.

https://www.vam.ac.uk/collections/gothic

Historic Context
Eyewitness Medieval Life by Andrew Langley

A medieval pilgrimage makes up the frame of Chaucer's Tales, but what was a pilgrimage? Chaucer shows us, but here are two articles that will provide details of the how and why people gathered for these long and often arduous journeys.

https://www.medievalists.net/2015/08/medieval-pilgrimages-its-all-about-the-journey/

https://www.metmuseum.org/toah/hd/pilg/hd_pilg.htm

In the feudal society of medieval times, everyone understood their social status or "estate." Read about "The Three Estates," and consider them as you read Chaucer's work. How do you think he feels about these estates?

http://cola.calpoly.edu/~dschwart/engl430/estates.html

The Crusades were a series of military campaigns with several motivations, including the European desire to reopen pilgrimage access to Holy Land sites associated with the life of Jesus. Read about the Crusades in your encyclopedia or online.

https://www.medievalists.net/2015/03/crusades-brief-history-1095-1500/

https://www.britannica.com/event/Crusades

You can take a virtual tour of Canterbury at this website:

https://www.hillside.co.uk/tour/tour.html

Assignment Schedule

Week 1

Begin reading the context resources and the poem, and follow the model in the Formats and Models chapter to write an Author Profile. You may find it helpful to use study questions as you think through the text. You will find thought-provoking questions at the links below or in CliffNotes. Be sure to refer to your writer's handbook if you have questions about grammar, structure, or style.

https://excellence-in-literature.com/chaucer-study-questions/

https://excellence-in-literature.com/study-questions-by-dr-wheeler/

Week 2

Model: A pilgrim in *Canterbury Tales*

Prompt: Choose one of the pilgrims, and using his or her voice and persona, write a letter to a friend describing the journey and telling about some of the other pilgrims and their stories. This does not have to be entirely in Middle English, but try to use a similar style of phrasing for your letter.

Week 3

Begin drafting a 750-word paper on the topic below. I recommend that you follow the writing process outlined in the "How to Write an Essay" chapter, consulting the models in the Formats and Models chapter and your writer's handbook as needed.

Model: Compare/Contrast Essay and MLA Format Model

Prompt: Compare the different functions of, attitudes toward, and/or adherence to the classical virtues in two or three of the pilgrims' tales. Consider ways in which each pilgrim's life role and appearance compares or contrasts with his or her actions and the story he or she tells.

Turn in the draft at the end of the week, so your writing mentor can evaluate it using the Content standards (Ideas/Concepts and Organization) on the rubric.

Week 4

Use the feedback on the rubric along with the writing mentor's comments to revise your paper. Before turning in the final draft, be sure you have addressed any issues marked on the evaluation rubric, and verify that the thesis is clear and your essay is well-organized. Use your writer's handbook to check grammar or punctuation so that your essay will be free from mechanical errors. Turn in the essay at the end of the week so that the writing mentor can use the evaluation rubric in the "How to Evaluate" chapter to check your work.

Module 4.3

Spenser, *Gawain,* and the Arthurian Legend

Fierce warres and faithfull loves shall moralize my song.

—*Faerie Queene.* Introduction. St. 1.

Focus Texts

Sir Gawain and the Green Knight (c. 1375–1400)

This story-poem has been translated by J. R. R. Tolkien and many others. The version in the *Norton Anthology* or almost any annotated version will do. Mass market paperbacks are not well annotated, so please avoid them.

To help you understand your reading, you may use the study questions provided by a college professor at:

http://cola.calpoly.edu/~dschwart/engl331/fq.html

The Faerie Queene (Book 1) by Edmund Spenser (c. 1552–1679)

Read the Letter to Raleigh and all the Faerie Queene Introductory Material at the EIL site, including the following:

INTRODUCTION:

I. The Age which produced *The Faerie Queene*

II. The Author of *The Faerie Queene*

III. Study of *The Faerie Queene*:

    1. A Romantic Epic

2. Influence of the New Learning

3. Interpretation of the Allegory

     (Pay special attention to the "Key to the Allegory" chart.)

4. The Spenserian Stanza

5. Versification

6. Diction and Style

IV. Chronological Table of Events

https://excellence-in-literature.com/faerie-queene-introductory-materials/

Read the twelve cantos of Book 1.

You may read these in an annotated version of *The Faerie Queene* (my favorite is edited by A. C. Hamilton) or at the link below. If you use the Gutenberg version, copy it to a text file (choose "select all" and "copy" from the file menu), format it, and print it out for easy reading and annotation.

http://www.gutenberg.org/ebooks/15272

Honors Text
Le Morte d'Arthur by Thomas Malory

Literary Period
Medieval: Middle English (Gawain)

Renaissance (Spenser)

Module Focus
The literary world is small, and in these two works we will observe how characters and motifs are used and reused across several centuries. We will also become better acquainted with the ideas of chivalry and honor, especially as they were expressed in the Arthurian legends.

Introduction
The legend of King Arthur is the common thread that runs through both selections for this module. The Arthurian legends have inspired poets and writers from the seventh century to the present. One of the first major authors to write about Arthur was Geoffrey of Monmouth in the twelfth-century *History of the Kings of*

Britain. Arthur is identified as a British king of the fifth or sixth century who united his people to resist the Saxon invasion. Countless other writers, such as Edmund Spenser and the author of *Sir Gawain*, have picked up the thread and continued to study and write about Arthur, just as we will be doing in this module.

Our first work, *Sir Gawain and the Green Knight*, is a medieval tale of chivalry and honor. It begins with a holiday feast at King Arthur's court, which is rudely interrupted by the challenge of a large green knight. Sir Gawain accepts the challenge, and the rest of the story details his experiences, temptations, and responses, showing the medieval concepts of honor and chivalry in action.

In *The Faerie Queene*, Edmund Spenser has created an allegorical tale in epic poetry. He planned to create a massive work of twelve books, with twelve cantos per book, each illustrating one of the "private moral virtues." He finished only six books, covering Holinesse, Temperaunce, Chastity, Friendship, Iustice, and Courtesie, before he died. As you see from the names of the virtues, the poem is written in a form of Middle English, so it, like Chaucer's massive work, will take a little patience to decipher, though it is not as difficult as it first appears.

There is much to consider in Spenser's masterpiece, since he has written within a very specific religious and political context. You will learn more about this in the introductory material that you will read before you begin the text. We will have time to study only the first book in this module, but if you enjoy it, feel free to continue on your own.

Something to think about . . .

C. S. Lewis and J. R. R. Tolkien were medieval scholars, steeped in the lore of Arthur, stories of Sir Gawain, the knights and fair ladies in *The Faerie Queene*, and the ancient myths and legends that were part of Britain's history. These legends helped to shape not only their stories, but the ideas and themes that run through their works. If you are not familiar with the Arthurian legends which lie at the root of many of these stories, you are likely to miss or misunderstand many of the themes and allusions you will find in the works of Lewis, Tolkien, and even Shakespeare. After this module I think you will appreciate the depth and richness of Tolkien and Lewis more than ever.

Be sure to notice . . .

Spenser wrote a letter to Sir Walter Raleigh "expounding his whole intention in the course of this worke." He identified *The Faerie Queene* as an allegory, stating that the general purpose of the twelve books is "to fashion a gentleman or noble person in vertuous and gentle discipline." He explains his use of King Arthur in this way: "I chose the historye of King Arthure, as most fitte for the excellency of his person, being made famous by many mens former workes, and also furthest from the daunger of envy, and suspition of present time …. I labour to pourtraict in Arthure, before he was king, the image of a brave knight, perfected in the twelve private morall vertues" (https://excellence-in-literature.com/letter-to-sir-walter-raleigh-by-edmund-spenser).

Rather than having Arthur serve as a central figure throughout his tales, Spenser chooses to focus on other knights, sending Arthur in only to rescue endangered heros or fair ladies. Spenser's skill at showing, rather than lecturing about, the chosen virtue allows him to tell vividly imaginative stories of knights, dragons, and other mythical creatures. Arthur appears briefly in each story, usually embodying the virtue that is the focus of that book. When you see him, be sure to consider how he is demonstrating a particular virtue.

Context Resources

Readings

Letter to Sir Walter Raleigh by Edmund Spenser

This interesting letter will help you understand Spenser's purpose in writing, as well as the historic and literary context of the book and the identity of the Faerie Queene. It will also provide a brief synopsis of the main plot of each of the first three books, explaining Spenser's choice of method—that of a "Poet historical" and not "an Historiographer." It is not long, but because of Spenser's archaic language, it can be a little confusing. You may copy it into a text file and print it out double-spaced, writing a translation into modern English beneath each line.

https://excellence-in-literature.com/letter-to-sir-walter-raleigh-by-edmund-spenser/

Was King Arthur a real person? Why has the story endured so long? And do the tales belong to the historical or romantic tradition? Dr. Hetta Howes addresses these questions and traces how the Arthurian legends have evolved over centuries to reflect various political, social, and literary interests.

https://excellence-in-literature.com/king-arthur-legends/ OR

https://www.bl.uk/medieval-literature/articles/the-legends-of-king-arthur

Dr. Judy Shoaf's thorough summary of the various King Arthur stories can help you understand why there are so many different versions of the Arthur story, how they are related, what they have in common, and who the key characters are.

https://people.clas.ufl.edu/jshoaf/arthurnet/arthur-from-scratch/

The Arthurian Legend website offers an overview of the legend and the books of Sir Thomas Malory's *Le Morte d'Arthur*.

https://www.arthurian-legend.com

The Luminarium site about *Sir Gawain and the Green Knight* offers critical essays, texts, books, and many good links.

http://www.luminarium.org/medlit/gawain.htm

Knights were to conduct themselves in accord with a code of conduct known as chivalry. This included, along with classical virtues, knightly piety, a warrior spirit, courtly manners, honor, and nobility.

https://www.newadvent.org/cathen/03691a.htm

See the definition of allegory from Ted Nellen's excellent Cyber English website:

http://www.tnellen.com/cybereng/lit_terms/allegory.html

Optional additional readings

Two good books you may find in your library are:

Chronicles of King Arthur by Andrea Hopkins is a fascinating, brief, scholarly overview of the Arthurian tales. The text is mostly taken from the original writers such as Thomas Malory and is seamlessly presented with a good selection of classic illustrations. I highly recommend this.

King Arthur and the Knights of the Round Table by Marcia Williams. This short book is a graphic introduction of the Arthurian legends. Each major character or event is featured in a double-page spread of pictures and text. You will probably find this in the children's section of the library.

The Arthurian Companion by Phyllis Ann Karr is a one-volume reference to all of the people and things related to Arthur. It is very handy, especially if you are reading Malory for the Honors option.

Want to read more about Arthur and the Knights of the Round Table? Here are a few other good retellings of the King Arthur legends.

- *The Story of King Arthur and his Knights* by Howard Pyle: a classic edition with delightful illustrations
- *King Arthur and His Knights* by Elizabeth Lodor Merchant
- *Sword at Sunset* by Rosemary Sutcliff
- *The Once and Future King* by T.H. White

The Author's Life

Edmund Spenser led an interesting life, and each of these short biographies highlights somewhat different parts of his life.

https://excellence-in-literature.com/edmund-spenser-biography/

http://www.luminarium.org/renlit/spensbio.htm

The Spenser Online site offers a timeline of Spenser's life.

http://core.ecu.edu/umc/Munster/biography.html

Poetry

The Idylls of the King by Alfred, Lord Tennyson

This cycle of twelve poems tells the Arthurian legends, mostly in blank verse. Although Tennyson's poem is not as long as *The Faerie Queene*, there are many similarities. Be sure to notice similarities and differences as you read. Which do you like better?

https://excellence-in-literature.com/idylls-of-the-king-by-tennyson/

Audio

If you have access through your local library or a streaming service to professional recordings of any of these works, I recommend using those. The amateur recordings from Librivox can have distracting quality issues that prevent full understanding or enjoyment.

For *The Faerie Queene*, you may want to listen to the audio book as you follow in the text. Sometimes hearing the story makes it more easily understood and enjoyed.

https://librivox.org/the-faerie-queene-book-1-by-edmund-spenser/

If your library does not have the King Arthur stories on CD, Librivox offers free audios of various versions.

Here is an abridged introduction to King Arthur:

http://librivox.org/king-arthur-and-his-knights-by-maude-l-radford/

Le Morte d'Arthur by Thomas Malory

https://librivox.org/le-morte-darthur-volume-1-by-sir-thomas-malory/

The Faerie Queene by Edmund Spenser is not complete at Librivox at the time of this writing, but you may listen to portions by visiting http://librivox.org/ and searching for the title.

Sir Gawain and the Green Knight

https://librivox.org/sir-gawain-and-the-green-knight-neilson-version/ or

https://librivox.org/gawayne-and-the-green-knight-by-charlton-miner-lewis

British writer Gordon Strong offers a fifty-plus-minute lecture on "King Arthur and the Mystical Landscape." This very informal talk begins with a madrigal; then Strong introduces what is known about Arthur as a historic and mythic figure. The recording takes a minute to start, but it's worth being patient for.

https://archive.org/details/king-arthur-gordon-strong

Music

Spenser would likely have been familiar with madrigals, a type of secular music from his era. Read about English madrigals, and listen to "The Nightengale" below and a few of the samples at *Umeå Akademiska Kör*. Scroll down the page to find the links to MP3 files.

https://excellence-in-literature.com/the-nightingale-english-madrigal/

http://www.acc.umu.se/~akadkor/early/IVM2.html

Spenser may have also heard compositions by his contemporary, composer William Byrd (c. 1540–1623). You may read a bit about Byrd and listen to a few examples here.

https://www.professorcarol.com/2020/04/03/byrd-ne-irascaris-voces8/

https://www.professorcarol.com/2019/03/08/byrd-miserere/

https://www.professorcarol.com/2016/07/29/byrd-pavan-galliard/

http://www.acc.umu.se/~akadkor/early/IVM7_Byrd_William.html

Video

Gawain and the Green Knight (1973) is a British film version of Sir Gawain. Although I have not seen it, some reviewers indicate that it sticks fairly close to the book. You will probably want to check your favorite movie guide to read more about it before seeing it. I cannot recommend other film versions of the story.

The Knights of the Round Table (1953) with Mel Ferrer and Ava Gardner. You may view a trailer at:

https://excellence-in-literature.com/knights-of-the-round-table-1953-movie-trailer/

Camelot is a 1967 musical based on the legend of King Arthur as told in *The Once and Future King*. With Richard Harris as King Arthur, the movie version won three Oscars. It is memorable, but you will want to read the reviews and decide whether it is suitable for your family.

http://www.imdb.com/title/tt0061439/

The Sword in the Stone is Disney's version of the King Arthur tale. It's based on T. H. White's The Once and Future King. I have not seen it, but it has been highly recommended to me.

https://excellence-in-literature.com/the-sword-in-the-stone-disney-movie-trailer

Visual Arts

Medieval stories were often told through visual arts. At the University of Rochester's Camelot Project, you can see illustrations from many different editions of the Arthurian legends. Which set of illustrations seems to best capture the essence of the story?

https://d.lib.rochester.edu/camelot/artists

A group of nineteenth-century artists known as the Pre-Raphaelites painted many romantic illustrations of Arthurian figures.

Queen Guenevere by William Morris

https://excellence-in-literature.com/arthurian-images-by-pre-raphaelites/

Guinevere-The Maying by Hon. John Collier

https://www.illusionsgallery.com/Guinevere.html

King Arthur by Charles Ernest Butler

https://www.illusionsgallery.com/King-Arthur-Butler.html

The Death of Arthur (Mort D'Arthur) by John Mulcaster Carrick

https://www.illusionsgallery.com/Death-Arthur-Carrick.html

Sir Galahad by George Frederic Watts

https://www.illusionsgallery.com/Galahad.html

Historic Context

To understand Spenser and the remarkable Elizabethan Age, read this interesting article by Dr. George Armstrong Wauchope.

https://excellence-in-literature.com/the-age-which-produced-the-faerie-queene/

Read about The Historical King Arthur at:

https://www.ancient.eu/article/1068/the-historical-king-arthur/

Read about the Middle Ages at:

https://www.britannica.com/topic/history-of-Europe/The-Middle-Ages

The 16th Century was one of incredible transformation and discovery. Read this informal overview and timeline.

http://www.lepg.org/sixteen.htm

https://www.cs.mcgill.ca/~rwest/wikispeedia/wpcd/wp/1/16th_century.htm

Glastonbury Abbey: "Over the years, the abbey has become the gravitational center of Britain's legendary universe, largely because of its role in the creation and development of the legends of Joseph of Arimathea and King Arthur …". Read about the Abbey's history and the two stories linked from the Myths and Legends page.

https://www.glastonburyabbey.com

https://www.glastonburyabbey.com/myths-legends.php

The Centering Spenser site from East Carolina University offers a look at Edmund Spenser's Irish castle, Kilcolman. You can see historic and current images of the castle and take a virtual tour.

http://core.ecu.edu/umc/Munster/index.html

Just for Fun

Here is a brief, interesting article on "How to Read and Speak Middle English."

http://www.ehow.com/how_8330816_speak-read-old-english.html

Visit the *Ancient Quest* website to find links about sword fighting and other medieval things (these links change, so we have not visited everything; please proceed with prudence).

http://www.ancientquest.com/links/links_a.html

What were people wearing when Spenser was alive in the 16th century? Visit the Fashion History Timeline to see.

https://fashionhistory.fitnyc.edu/category/16th-century/

Assignment Schedule

Week 1

Read *Sir Gawain and the Green Knight*, Spenser's letter to Raleigh, and the Arthurian background readings. Follow the model in the Formats and Models chapter to write an Author Profile on Spenser. Be sure to refer to your writer's handbook if you have questions about grammar, structure, or style.

Week 2

Write an approach paper on *Sir Gawain and the Green Knight* using the instructions and samples in the Formats and Models chapter.

Get acquainted with *The Faerie Queene* by going through the book and copying all the epigraphs or "Arguments" at the beginning of each canto. These four-line poetic stanzas summarize the events of the canto and identify most of the main characters in the action. Make sure you understand them, writing a paraphrase or sketching illustrations if necessary.

Week 3

Begin drafting a 750-word paper on one of the topics below. I recommend that you follow the writing process outlined in the "How to Write an Essay" chapter, consulting the models in the Formats and Models chapter and your writer's handbook as needed.

1- Model: Literary Analysis Essay and MLA Format Model

Prompt: Consider the ideal of knighthood as presented in Sir Gawain, the Red Crosse Knight, and in Arthur. In what ways do each of these men embody the ideal knight, and in what ways does he fail to live up to that ideal? Does it seem that Spenser and the author of *Sir Gawain* support or critique the traditional, chivalric ideal? Use quotes from the text to support your thesis.

2- Model: Poetry Analysis Essay and MLA Format Model

Prompt: Analyze the figurative language used in book 1, canto 1, stanzas 7–14. Pay particular attention to the ways in which the figurative language indicates that all is not as it seems, especially in connection with the setting. Also, look at how the Red Crosse Knight has a difficult time distinguishing appearance from reality.

Alternate Assignment

Rewrite each of the twelve cantos of Book 1 of *The Faerie Queene* in prose. Tell the story with colorful details, making sure that your reader will finish the tale with a vivid understanding of the characters and events. Make this as long as necessary in order to tell a good story.

Turn in the draft at the end of the week, so your writing mentor can evaluate it using the Content standards (Ideas/Concepts and Organization) on the rubric.

Week 4

Use the feedback on the rubric along with the writing mentor's comments to revise your paper. Before turning in the final draft, be sure you have addressed any issues marked on the evaluation rubric, and verify that the thesis is clear and your essay is well-organized. Use your writer's handbook to check grammar or punctuation so that your essay will be free from mechanical errors. Turn in the essay at the end of the week so that the writing mentor can use the evaluation rubric in the "How to Evaluate" chapter to check your wor.

Module 4.4

King Lear by William Shakespeare (1564–1616)

How sharper than a serpent's tooth it is to have a thankless child!

—Act I, Scene IV

Focus Text

King Lear by William Shakespeare

You will need the text, as well as a video, of this play. You can find it in a Shakespeare anthology or as a stand-alone book—I recommend the Ignatius Critical Edition.

Honors Text

Hamlet by William Shakespeare

Literary Period

Renaissance

Module Focus

We will see the classic elements of tragedy at work and consider the significance of the Gloucester sub-plot to the unity of the play.

Introduction

Shakespeare's tragedies can be hard to read. It is not just because the plays are written in King James English; it is because Shakespeare shows so clearly how one man's lapse in judgment can start a chain of events that leads to disaster and death for many. However, Shakespeare illustrates the stark truth that we reap what we sow—and often, so do the people who love us. The truth that makes this play challenging may make it a play that's hard to enjoy the first time around, but you'll find it's also a story that you will never forget.

Something to think about . . .

Lear is a classic tragic hero who comes to a disastrous end through his own actions but also grows and changes in the process. As you read through *King Lear,* observe his character from beginning to end. Although the act of dividing his kingdom is unwise, it is clear from the loyalty of his friends and the love of his daughter, Cordelia, that Lear was much more than a fool; he was a great man, brought low. His change of circumstance is accompanied by new self-knowledge and a change of heart which allows him to humbly accept his fate.

Be sure to notice . . .

William Shakespeare, a playwright and poet of the late sixteenth century, remains one of the greatest writers of all time. During the fifty-two years of his life, he wrote thirty-nine plays and many poems. Many of his plays are still performed on stages around the world, and lines from his works are found throughout our language. As you read King Lear, watch for lines or phrases that sound familiar. Shakespeare is everywhere!

Context Resources

Readings

"Enjoying *King Lear*" is Dr. Ed Friedlander's insightful introduction to the play. Friedlander is a pathologist, not a professor, but his lifelong study and appreciation for Shakespeare's masterpiece illuminates *Lear* better than any other introduction I have seen. Don't miss this.

http://www.pathguy.com/kinglear.html

There are many stories of hubris in ancient literature, including an early version of "The Emperor's New Clothes" from the 14th century. Another brief, well-known tale of hubris is the story of King Nebuchadnezzar in Daniel 4 in the Bible. Like most people of his time, Shakespeare was familiar with both scripture and ancient literature, and freely borrowed and adapted plot elements for his plays. Read both of these stories and keep them in mind as you are reading *King Lear.*

Notice parallels between the stories and consider why hubris remains a temptation when it is so clearly destructive.

https://andersen.sdu.dk/vaerk/hersholt/TheEmperorsNewClothes_e.html

The introduction to *King Lear* in the *Norton Shakespeare* (by Stephen Greenblatt, et al) is another excellent resource. If you have access to this anthology, read this introduction before reading the play.

This delightful introduction to Shakespeare's Grammar will help you understand his writings much more easily.

https://www.bardweb.net/content/grammar/grammar.html

Charles and Mary Lamb rewrote all of Shakespeare's plays, for children. You will probably find their *Tales from Shakespeare* at your local library, or you can read it online. If you read this short version before seeing the video or reading the full-length play, you will have a much better idea of what is happening. I recommend it. Here is the Lambs' short version of *King Lear*:

https://excellence-in-literature.com/excellence-in-lit/
tales-from-shakespeare-by-charles-and-mary-lamb-king-lear

Shakespeare's Food Poesies. Food shows up in many places in Shakespeare's dramas, and this site offers an alphabetically organized encyclopedia of quotes. It is an interesting way to see what was included in the Elizabethan diet. Here are the O and C entries to the list; you can find other letters with site search function if you are interested.

http://soupsong.com/qbardo.html

http://soupsong.com/qbardc.html

Penguin Classics *Teachers' Guide*: If you don't have the Ignatius Critical Edition of *King Lear* (preferred option); read the Introduction, Overview, Elements of Tragedy, Historical Context, and Shakespeare's Language in this guide from Penguin.

https://www.penguin.com/static/pdf/teachersguides/kinglear.pdf

The Author's Life

Shakespeare by Peter Chrisp: This Eyewitness book, published by Dorling Kindersley, is a superb guide to Shakespeare and his plays. Like most Eyewitness books, it is lavishly illustrated, and both entertaining and informative.

https://amzn.to/3oql6x2

The Shakespeare Resource Center provides a good introductory biography of Shakespeare, as well as many other useful resources.

http://www.bardweb.net/man.html

Timeline of important events in Shakespeare's life

https://absoluteshakespeare.com/trivia/timeline/timeline.htm

The Seven Ages of Shakespeare's Life

https://internetshakespeare.uvic.ca/Library/SLT/life/index.html

The Shakespeare Resource Center provides a good introductory biography of Shakespeare, as well as many other useful resources.

https://www.bardweb.net/index.html

Who wrote Shakespeare's works? Now that you have read about Shakespeare, you should know that there has been a controversy about who actually wrote all his works. The Shakespeare Oxford site offers "Shakespeare Authorship 101" which is strongly rebutted at the entertaining Oxfraud and at The Shakespeare Authorship Page. After reading some of the articles on these sites, what do you think?

https://shakespeareoxfordfellowship.org/discover-shakespeare/

https://oxfraud.com and https://shakespeareauthorship.com/#featured

Poetry

Read poetry from Shakespeare's contemporaries, including Queen Elizabeth, Sir Philip Sydney, and Sir Walter Raleigh. Can you see common themes or styles among them?

https://excellence-in-literature.com/poetry-by-shakespeare-contemporaries/

Besides his plays, Shakespeare wrote a good deal of poetry, including many sonnets. Read at least three more poems from the links below:

https://rpo.library.utoronto.ca/poets/shakespeare-william

Audio

Your library may have this play on CD, but you can also find professional and free versions online. Here are two options.

https://amzn.to/3v86L6P

https://librivox.org/king-lear-by-william-shakespeare/

Music

Music of the Renaissance. This website by California State Polytechnic University, Pomona offers free MIDI files of Renaissance music organized by composer. You can listen to music of the sort Shakespeare might have heard! Just click and listen—it makes great background music for reading *King Lear.*

http://www.curtisclark.org/emusic/renaissa.html

King Lear Overture by Hector Berlioz is a beautiful piece inspired by *King Lear.* You may listen at the link below or look for a recording at your local library.

https://excellence-in-literature.com/shakespeare-resources/

The musical score for the *King Lear Overture* takes a little while to load, but if you are musically inclined, you may enjoy following along while listening to the piece.

https://musopen.org/music/8741-grande-ouverture-du-roi-lear-h-53/

Video

Because *King Lear* is a play, you must watch it in order to fully understand it. I suggest watching it first with subtitles, as the fast pace of the play and its Shakespearean English can make it easy to lose the thread of the narrative.

https://amzn.to/2OfTkB5

https://excellence-in-literature.com/king-lear-excerpt/

Visual Arts

Photographs and artwork will help you visualize Shakespeare's life, as well as the setting and characters of *King Lear.*

Shakespeare Birthplace Photographs

https://www.shakespeare.org.uk/visit/shakespeares-birthplace/

Painting: *King Lear and the Fool in the Storm* by William Dyce

https://www.nationalgalleries.org/art-and-artists/30951/king-lear-and-fool-storm

The Awakening of King Lear by Robert Smirke

https://www.folger.edu/painting-shakespeare/robert-smirke-awakening-of-king-lear

Painting: *King Lear and Cordelia* by Benjamin West

https://emuseum.huntington.org/objects/198/meeting-of-lear-and-cordelia

Ford Madox Brown's Drawings for *King Lear*. An amazing, graphic story!

http://www.english.emory.edu/classes/Shakespeare_Illustrated/Brown%27sLear.html

Copies of engravings illustrating scenes from *King Lear*

https://absoluteshakespeare.com/pictures/king_lear.htm

Links to more artwork depicting scenes from *King Lear*

http://english.emory.edu/classes/Shakespeare_Illustrated/LearPaintings.html

Historical Context

The *Life in Elizabethan England* site, created by writer Maggie Pierce Secara, offers links so that you can explore interesting details of Elizabethan England, including fashion, household management, heraldry, education, occupations, and more.

http://elizabethan.org/compendium/

These two pages offer slightly different coverage of the ideas and living conditions of Elizabethan England.

https://www.britainexpress.com/History/Elizabethan_life.htm

http://www.localhistories.org/tudor.html

Religion was a major topic in 16th-Century England and its issues and language appear throughout Shakespeare's work. The profound changes that occurred during the 16th century are explored in the two articles from the National Park Service and BBC sites below.

https://www.nps.gov/fora/learn/education/unit-1-the-church-of-england-in-the-sixteenth-century.htm

https://www.bbc.co.uk/bitesize/guides/znjnb9q/revision/1

Shakespeare's Globe Theatre offers a virtual tour plus lots of other learning resources to help you understand Shakespeare and his work.

https://www.shakespearesglobe.com/learn/teaching-resources/

Assignment Schedule

Week 1

Begin reading the context resources and watch the *King Lear* video. Follow the model in the Formats and Models chapter to write an Author Profile. Be sure to refer to your writer's handbook if you have questions about grammar, structure, or style.

Week 2

Read through *King Lear,* considering the questions below. As you read, you will come across words that are unfamiliar. Write them down, along with the act and scene number, so you can look them up later. Note that the following scenes are particularly important to the development of the plot, and mark them so that you may return to them as you are writing your essay.

- Scenes 1.1 and 1.2 establish the plot and begin to shape the various themes and motifs, as well as the plot and the parallel subplot together. Also pay particular attention to 1.4, 2.4, 3.2, 3.4, 3.6, 3.7, 4.1, 4.6, 4.7, and 5.3.
- What parallels do you see between Gloucester and Lear and their children?
- Think about the language of sight and blindness throughout the play. How does it contribute to the development of the story?
- Analyze the theme of fate versus choice in the play. Does Shakespeare seem to attribute the things that happen to his characters more to fate, or to choice? What do you think?
- Notice how irony and paradox are a part of tragedy.

As you read through the play, use the instructions for the Summary portion of the Approach Paper to write a brief summary of each scene. Number each summary with the scene number so that you can use your summary to find examples you wish to quote in your essay.

Week 3

Begin drafting a 750-word paper on the topic below. I recommend that you follow the writing process outlined in the "How to Write an Essay" chapter, consulting the models in the Formats and Models chapter and your writer's handbook as needed.

Model: Model: Compare/Contrast Essay and MLA Format Model

Prompt: Compare and contrast Gloucester and Lear, focusing on their choices, their adherence to kingly or noble ideals, their relationships with their children, their level of wisdom and humility (at the beginning and at the end of the story), and/ or other parallels you find interesting. Be sure to integrate quotes from the text to support your comparisons.

For additional assistance, you may refer to your writer's handbook or the "How to Write a Compare/Contrast Essay" article at

https://excellence-in-literature.com/resources-for-teaching/
how-to-write-a-compare-contrast-essay

Turn in the draft at the end of the week, so your writing mentor can evaluate it using the Content standards (Ideas/Concepts and Organization) on the rubric.

Week 4

Use the feedback on the rubric along with the writing mentor's comments to revise your paper. Before turning in the final draft, be sure you have addressed any issues marked on the evaluation rubric, and verify that the thesis is clear and your essay is well-organized. Use your writer's handbook to check grammar or punctuation so that your essay will be free from mechanical errors. Turn in the essay at the end of the week so that the writing mentor can use the evaluation rubric in the "How to Evaluate" chapter to check your wor.

Module 4.5

Paradise Lost by John Milton (1608–1674)

> *. . . What in me is dark*
> *Illumine, what is low raise and support,*
> *That to the height of this great argument*
> *I may assert eternal Providence,*
> *And justify the ways of God to men.*
>
> —*Paradise Lost.* Book i. Line 22

Focus Text

Paradise Lost by John Milton

I recommend *The Major Works* by John Milton (Oxford World's Classics) for this challenging work.

Dartmouth College offers an annotated online edition at this site, but please don't try to read the entire work online. The only thing you might want to use this for is to quickly click on unfamiliar classical references if you're reading from an edition that lacks good notes.

http://www.dartmouth.edu/~milton/reading_room/pl/book_1/text.shtml

Honors Text

Dr. Faustus by Christopher Marlowe or

Confessions by St. Augustine of Hippo (Ignatius Press edition)

Literary Period

Renaissance

Module Focus

As you read through the poem, consider how Milton uses epic characteristics and techniques. Be able to make brief, basic comparisons with how Spenser and the *Beowulf* poet have used them. (The characteristics of the epic are listed in the module on *Beowulf*.)

Introduction

John Milton's masterwork tells an epic tale of rebellion, war, and the fall from grace, and the loss of paradise. Encompassing the greatest ideals of both Renaissance and Reformation, the poem has been described as second only to Shakespeare's writings in its influence on English literature. Milton was exceptionally widely read and he draws upon history, the Greek and Latin classics, and the Bible for the many allusions in his work.

Something to think about . . .

Milton has chosen to use the grand classical style for his epic. This places his work in the tradition of Homer and Virgil, whose works we will study in *World Literature*. His use of classical imagery such as Orpheus (sleep) or Cynthia (the moon) makes it a little more challenging to read, so if you are reading a version that is not well annotated, I encourage you to use a dictionary of allusions or the Dartmouth online version to look up allusions if you are not using a good annotated edition. Milton also appears in his own work as the narrator. How does this affect the story? Does it make it seem more plausible?

Be sure to notice . . .

Here's another epic poem in the tradition of Homer, Virgil, and Chaucer. Notice the differences between the medieval style of *Beowulf*, Chaucer, and the Renaissance style of Spenser and Milton. Why do you think that each author chose the poetic form to tell these great stories?

Context Resources

Readings

Genesis 1–3: Read these three chapters, which are the source for Milton's story. You may read this in the same translation as Milton would have used (first link), and you may even see Milton's own Bible in the British Library's online archive (second link).

https://www.kingjamesbibleonline.org/1611-Bible/

https://www.bl.uk/collection-items/john-miltons-family-bible

The Tale of Paradise Lost: Based on the Poem by John Milton by Jude Daly and Nancy Willard: This brief overview of the poem can orient you to the characters and basic plot line of the poem.

https://amzn.to/37QhkkQ

Darkness Visible is a Milton site put together by students or graduates from Christ's College, Cambridge. These Milton enthusiasts have put together a great in-depth site that explores many different aspects of *Paradise Lost* and John Milton's life. I recommend that you read most of this site, beginning with the introduction, and exploring the "Paradise Lost," "Contexts," "Influence," and "Milton and the Arts" links from the navigation bar at the top.

https://darknessvisible.christs.cam.ac.uk/intro/introduction.html

The Norton Anthology of British Literature offers an introduction to Milton's *Paradise Lost* and the classical themes that influenced Milton. If you do not have that available, the *Paradise Lost* website provides a helpful overview, a look at some of the classic illustrations, and other helpful background information.

https://www.paradiselost.org/novel.html

The Luminarium site has interesting and well-researched articles on John Milton. You will find a biography, texts, quotes, criticism, illustrations, links, books, and more.

http://www.luminarium.org/sevenlit/milton/

Dictionary of Allusions: If you do not have a well annotated version of *Paradise Lost*, you will need a dictionary of allusions, which you can find at the library, bookstore, or online (search at http://books.google.com/).

Blackwell Publishing offers a scholarly magazine called the *Milton Quarterly Journal* that publishes articles on all things Milton. Not many poets can boast of being the feature subject of an entire magazine, especially 400 years after their death! You may download a free sample issue.

https://onlinelibrary.wiley.com/journal/1094348x

The Silva Rhetoricae site is one of my favorite places for learning about classical rhetoric. It's written by a university professor who loves his subject and knows it well. Read at least the sections on "What is Rhetoric" and "Encompassing Terms," including the individual word definitions linked in the text.

http://rhetoric.byu.edu

The Author's Life

If you find Milton especially fascinating, you may want to read a full-length biography such as *The Life of John Milton: A Critical Biography* by Barbara K. Lewalski.

Read any good, brief biography of Milton from your library, or in an encyclopedia, or at one or more of the sites below.

https://excellence-in-literature.com/john-milton-biography/

http://www.luminarium.org/sevenlit/milton/miltonbio.htm

https://www.biography.com/writer/john-milton

Poetry

You may read a few key Milton poems on the EIL site, including two that reveal Milton's spiritual struggle with his early loss of sight in "On His Blindness" and his grief at the death of a friend in the lengthy pastoral elegy "Lycidas."

https://excellence-in-literature.com/john-milton-poems/

Milton's friend, Andrew Marvell , wrote a poem, "On Mr. Milton's 'Paradise Lost'," describing his reaction to the work. To read Marvell's poem, go to

https://excellence-in-literature.com/on-mr-miltons-paradise-lost-by-andrew-marvell

Another of Milton's contemporaries, George Herbert (1593–1633), wrote some of the most beautiful, accessible poetry of the time. You may read "Gratefullnesse" and "Easter Wings," two of my favorites among his poems, linked from the George

Herbert Poetry page at EIL. Be sure to especially note the shape of the poem "Easter Wings."

https://excellence-in-literature.com/george-herbert-poetry

https://rpo.library.utoronto.ca/poets/herbert-george

If you enjoy Herbert's poetry, you will want to read *Working it Out: Growing Spiritually with the Poetry of George Herbert* by Joseph L. Womack. This delightful volume offers an explication of 51 Herbert poems. For each poem he covers The Big Picture, The Parts of the Picture, The Parts of the Picture Come Together, Reflections, and Scriptures for Further Reflection. It is a helpful guide to getting the most from reading any poetry, and it's available from EverydayEducation. com.

Do you enjoy memorizing poetry? Can you imagine memorizing anything as long as *Paradise Lost*? Professor and actor John Basinger memorized all twelve books of the poem over a period of nine years. Perhaps reading about it will inspire you to memorize a poem that you like.

https://nautil.us/blog/-this-man-memorized-a-60000_word-poem-using-deep-encoding

https://www.doingwhatmatters.com/how-to-memorize/

Audio

Like most great epic poems, *Paradise Lost* is meant to be heard. Listen to the brief sample of Paradise Lost, performed by Ian Richardson, at the first link below. You can get the entire professionally narrated version from online bookstores and some libraries, or you may listen to a free amateur version from Librivox.

https://excellence-in-literature.com/john-milton-poems/

https://amzn.to/2ZTDqhZ

https://librivox.org/paradise-lost-by-john-milton-2/

Yale University Professor John Rogers has recently posted a series of lectures on Milton and *Paradise Lost* at Open Yale Courses. I have not gotten all the way through them yet, but what I have heard so far is very interesting. This seems to be an excellent secular resource. To watch these video lectures, click on the

Sessions link near the top of the page; I suggest that you skip past the first sessions, and go directly to the Paradise Lost lectures (9–20).

https://oyc.yale.edu/english/engl-220

Music

Christ's College at Cambridge University presents an outstanding essay on "Milton and Music," detailing Milton's interest and ability, and listing musical works that are inspired by or based upon his writing, including "Samson" by George Frederic Handel. You may listen to a piece from the "Samson" opera at the second link.

https://darknessvisible.christs.cam.ac.uk/music.html

https://excellence-in-literature.com/let-the-bright-seraphim-by-handel/

You may listen to more of Handel's music from online streaming services.

Video

This staging of *Paradise Lost* is based on speeches from the epic. They are presented in the order found in the poem.

https://miltonrevealed.berkeley.edu/videos/john-miltons-paradise-lost-drama-part-1

Read through the Cambridge University page on "Milton and Performance" to read about the issues faced in producing *Paradise Lost* as a play, opera, or movie.

https://darknessvisible.christs.cam.ac.uk/performance.html

Visual Arts

Paradise Lost has inspired stunning artwork by artists such as Gustav Dore, Peter Breughel the Elder, Tintoretto, William Blake, and Michelangelo. You may view Dore's illustrations at the University at Buffalo digital archives.

https://digital.lib.buffalo.edu/items/browse/tag/Paradise+Lost

Historical Context

John Milton's life spanned the years before and after the English Civil Wars. He was an outspoken proponent of a republican, rather than a monarchical form of government, and wrote extensively on the subject. Because of his prolific pamphleteering, including pamphlets arguing in favor of divorce and the necessity for the execution of Charles I. Because of his "regicide tracts," Milton's life was in jeopardy when the monarchy was restored after the war, and he lost his government job and was imprisoned for a time.

Read about the English Civil Wars and Oliver Cromwell in "The turbulent 17th century: Civil War, regicide, the Restoration and the Glorious Revolution."

https://www.bl.uk/restoration-18th-century-literature/articles/the-turbulent-17th-century-civil-war-regicide-the-restoration-and-the-glorious-revolution

What was the "Rump Parliament"? Learn about it here, and consider whether something like it could happen in your country.

http://bcw-project.org/church-and-state/the-commonwealth/rump-parliament

Milton was an ardent supporter of Oliver Cromwell, the English general who led armies of the Parliament of England against King Charles I during the English Civil War and ruled the British Isles as Lord Protector from 1653 until his death in 1658. Why do you think he appealed to Milton?

https://www.historic-uk.com/HistoryUK/HistoryofEngland/Oliver-Cromwell/

Milton's Political Context

https://darknessvisible.christs.cam.ac.uk/politics.html

Protestant and Catholic Reformations:* It is important to understand the Reformations as a historical context for Milton's writings. Read about them and one of their unexpected consequences at the references below:

https://excellence-in-literature.com/the-protestant-reformation-by-steven-kreis/

http://www.historyguide.org/earlymod/lecture5c.html

https://voxeu.org/article/protestant-reformation-and-allocation-resources-europe

Milton's Religious Context*

https://darknessvisible.christs.cam.ac.uk/religion.html

*NOTE: As always, we are approaching these two resources from a historical and biographical perspective; not in a sectarian way.

The Renaissance was another important influence on Milton's work. Read about it in your encyclopedia or at the resources below:

Eyewitness Renaissance by Alison Cole

https://www.britannica.com/event/Renaissance

http://www.historyworld.net/wrldhis/PlainTextHistories.asp?historyid=ac88

https://excellence-in-literature.com/renaissance/

https://excellence-in-literature.com/history-of-the-renaissance-by-bamber-gascoigne/

Places to Go

If you are in England, you may want to tour Milton's cottage in Buckinghamshire. You may see photos and read more about it at the website:

https://www.miltonscottage.org

Assignment Schedule

Week 1

Begin reading the context resources and follow the model in the Formats and Models chapter to write an Author Profile. Begin watching, listening to, and/or reading *Paradise Lost*. Be sure to refer to your writer's handbook if you have questions about grammar, structure, or style.

Week 2

Continue studying the focus work and context resources (you may add more weeks to this module if needed). Consider the following ideas as you read:

- Note how Milton has used images of light and darkness to convey specific ideas throughout the poem.

- Before the fall Adam spends a great deal of time in contemplation of God, while Satan spends his time in contemplation of himself. Consider the significance of this.

- How do Milton's images of hell portray the truth about the nature of evil?

- Consider Milton's portrayal of knowledge, free will, and independence in the poem. Can you see ways in which the ideas of the Renaissance and the Protestant Reformation may have shaped Milton's perspective?

- Notice how the descriptions of Eve and Satan echo one another. What do they have in common?

- In the first two books, be sure to notice the contrast between Satan's grand posturing and the reality of his evil schemes and ultimate failure (he may have won a battle, but he will not win the war).

- Note how books 9–10 show the effects of sin and portray the way in which humans fall.

- By the end of Milton's story, can you tell what he believes about pride, sin, and repentance?

As you watch, listen to, or read *Paradise Lost*, use the instructions for the Summary portion of the Approach Paper to write a brief, interesting summary (up to 300 words) of each book, noting the principal events and characters. Select a quotation from the book itself or from the Bible, or even from another source, to use as an epigraph for each of your summaries.

Week 3

Begin drafting a 750-word paper on the topic below. I recommend that you follow the writing process outlined in the "How to Write an Essay" chapter, consulting the models in the Formats and Models chapter and your writer's handbook as needed.

1- Model: Literary Analysis Essay and MLA Format Model

Prompt: Consider the ways in which goodness and evil are depicted in *Paradise Lost*, paying particular attention to the historical and social context of the work (the Protestant Reformation and the Renaissance). Use brief textual quotes to support your thesis.

2- Model: Compare/Contrast Essay and MLA Format Model

Prompt: Consider the definition of the epic form, and compare and contrast the ways in which the assigned portions of *Paradise Lost* compare as epic with either the assigned portions of *The Faerie Queene* or *Beowulf*. You probably will have to focus on two or three epic characteristics that lead to a fruitful comparison.

Turn in the draft at the end of the week, so your writing mentor can evaluate it using the Content standards (Ideas/Concepts and Organization) on the rubric.

Week 4

Use the feedback on the rubric along with the writing mentor's comments to revise your paper. Before turning in the final draft, be sure you have addressed any issues marked on the evaluation rubric and verify that the thesis is clear and your essay is well-organized. Use your writer's handbook to check grammar or punctuation so that your essay will be free from mechanical errors. Turn in the essay at the end of the week so that the writing mentor can use the evaluation rubric in the "How to Evaluate" chapter to check your work.

Module 4.6

Pride and Prejudice by Jane Austen (1775–1817)

It is a truth universally acknowledged,
that a single man in possession of a good fortune,
must be in want of a wife.

—Jane Austen

Focus Text

Pride and Prejudice by Jane Austen

I recommend the edition by Ignatius Critical Editions for its insightful introduction and commentary.

Honors Texts

Sense and Sensibility or other novel by Jane Austen

Middlemarch by George Eliot

Literary Period

Neoclassical/Romantic

Module Focus

You will become familiar with Regency England, Romantic and Neoclassical literary periods, and how Jane Austen skillfully melded the ideas of one period into the style of another. You will also meet some of the poets of the era and see how they embodied the ideas of the Romantic era.

Introduction

It is not easy to explain why *Pride and Prejudice* is one of the most popular novels of all time. The plot, after all, does not involve sweeping drama, earthshaking events, or even spellbinding suspense. Why do people read Jane Austen's masterpiece, not just once, but time after time? I believe it is because of Jane herself—her delightful wit, her interesting (sometimes aggravating) characters, and her enduring themes. Like Shakespeare, she reveals truths about human nature that ring true despite cultural changes. Her books are subtle; like shortbread cookies, the first bite may seem bland, especially if you are used to something bold and splashy. By the time you finish, however, chances are that you will want more. Enjoy!

Something to think about . . .

Nearly two hundred years after her death, there are active Jane Austen societies in several countries, and her novels remain favorites for book clubs and reading circles. Why have these novels stood the test of time? What are the characteristics that have kept them fresh and interesting for generations of readers? Do you think it is the plots, settings, characters, themes, or a combination of these?

Be sure to notice . . .

One of the primary characteristics of Jane Austen's novels is their subtle wit. As you read, be sure to note the humor in Austen's dialogue. How does this help to reveal a character's personality, and how does it enhance the storyline?

Context Resources

Readings

PBS Masterpiece Theatre offers a section devoted to Jane Austen and her works. It
   includes a timeline a, film clips, including behind the scenes excerpts, a page for
   each book, and a nice selection of resources for further research.

   https://www.pbs.org/wgbh/masterpiece/
   specialfeatures/a-guide-to-jane-austens-novels/#

Jane Austen's *History of England*: On its *Turning the Pages* website, the British
   Library offers an interactive version of *The History of England*, handwritten by
   Austen when she was 15. This is a funny parody of history books of the time,
   and well worth reading. The book is available online in both an interactive and a
   non-interactive version. The interactive version (first link) allows you to virtually

turn the pages, move a magnifying glass over the page, and listen to an audio recording of the text. The non-interactive version (second link) is better for a slow connection, and you can still listen to the audio and see enlarged images of the pages.

http://www.bl.uk/turning-the-pages/

http://www.bl.uk/onlinegallery/ttp/austen/accessible/introduction.html

Pemberley.com offers an annotated listing of characters, with genealogical charts for each book.

https://pemberley.com/janeinfo/ppdrmtis.html

If you enjoy Austen and her works, you may want to join the Jane Austen Society of North America. If offers an entertaining blog plus essay and filmmaking competitions.

http://www.jasna.org

The Author's Life

At the library, look for Deirdre Le Faye's *Jane Austen,* part of the outstanding British Writer's Lives series. If you cannot find it, the online biographies will do.

https://excellence-in-literature.com/jane-austen-biography/

Jane Austen's nephew wrote one of the first biographies of his famous aunt. Look for it at your library, or read it online.

http://labrocca.com/ja/index.html

Here are other Austen biographies online:

http://www.pemberley.com/janeinfo/janelife.html

http://www.victorianweb.org/previctorian/austen/bio.html

What did Jane Austen and her characters read? Here's a list of her literary allusions.

https://pemberley.com/janeinfo/litallus.html

If you have access to *The Politically Incorrect Guide to English and American Literature* by Elizabeth Kantor, PhD (available through libraries or bookstores), Read the section on Jane Austen. Kantor offers a fascinating look at Austen's world and thoroughly debunks the notion that Austen is a feminist writer.

Poetry

Some of the greatest British Romantic writers were poets, and reading their work can help you gain a clearer picture of the conventions of Romanticism. Be sure to review the brief synopsis of Romanticism in this study guide and read the brief poet biographies linked from each poetry page.

William Blake

From *Songs of Innocence and of Experience*: "Introduction" (read two poems, one at the beginning of 'Innocence,' one at the beginning of 'Experience')

- "The Ecchoing Green"
- "Earth's Answer"
- "The Divine Image"

https://excellence-in-literature.com/william-blake-poetry/

William Wordsworth

- "Lines Composed a Few Miles Above Tintern Abbey"
- "Ode: Intimations of Immortality"
- "The World is Too Much With Us"
- "Surprised by Joy"

https://excellence-in-literature.com/william-wordsworth-poems/

Samuel Taylor Coleridge

- "Kubla Khan"
- "Dejection: An Ode"

https://excellence-in-literature.com/poems-by-samuel-taylor-coleridge/

Percy Bysshe Shelley

- "Mont Blanc"
- "Ozymandius"
- "Ode to the West Wind"

https://excellence-in-literature.com/percy-bysshe-shelley-poems/

John Keats

- "Ode to a Nightingale"

- "Ode on Melancholy"

  https://excellence-in-literature.com/john-keats-poetry/

Audio

Your library may have this novel on CD, but it is also available on streaming services and as an amateur recording from Librivox.

  https://amzn.to/3q4W4hE

  https://librivox.org/pride-and-prejudice-by-jane-austen-3/

Music

The music of Regency England has a very distinctive sound, with an emphasis on stringed instruments. This period includes folk and classical music by composers such as Henry Purcell. Listen to a few samples of his music below.

  https://www.bbc.co.uk/programmes/p02gd95l

At the Regency Ballroom, you can hear English Country Dance music from the era of Jane Austen. The second link presents more details on what types of dances Jane Austen and her characters actually would have danced.

  https://www.bfv.com/regency/

  https://www.kickery.com/2009/11/what-did-jane-austen-dance.html

English country dancing is somewhat similar to square dancing, and it's an amazing amount of fun and good exercise. If you've never tried it, the third link below offers a brief introduction from the English Folk Dance and Song Society.

  https://youtu.be/uzlmpst99Fk

Video

I highly recommend the 1995 BBC/A&E version of *Pride and Prejudice,* with Colin Firth and Jennifer Ehle. It incorporates much of Austen's incomparable dialogue and remains generally faithful to the novel. You may view more information and a few clips at the BBC site.

  http://www.bbc.co.uk/drama/prideandprejudice/episodes/

You may enjoy watching this brief trailer of the 1995 version, put together by a fan:

  https://excellence-in-literature.com/1995-pride-and-prejudice-fan-trailer/

Jane Austen's *Life, Society, Works* is a DVD program by the UK film company, Artsmagic, Ltd. This delightful introduction to Austen and her works uses photographs, video footage of the lovely British countryside, and her letters to provide a very personal overview of her world. This is well worth watching.

https://amzn.to/3kBy8B2

Visual Arts

Jane Austen's literary style reflects the order and symmetry of the Neoclassical period. You may see examples of Neoclassical paintings in an art history book or at this website (click on artist portraits to view examples of their work).

https://www.wikiart.org/en/artists-by-art-movement/neoclassicism

Take a look at "Notes and illustrations on Regency clothing styles (with 1895 Charles E. Brock illustrations for *Pride and Prejudice*)." This will help you picture Austen and her characters.

https://pemberley.com/janeinfo/ppbrokil.html

Historical Context

Jane Austen's England, by Maggie Lane and Robert Hale

The problems encountered by the characters in Pride and Prejudice may seem far-fetched and entirely unlikely if you don't understand the social background of this era in English history. As you will see when you read the book, life was much different from what a twentieth-century person is likely to experience. Read the article below to understand what Jane's world was like.

https://excellence-in-literature.com/
social-background-of-pride-and-prejudice-by-pamela-whalan/

Jane Austen was on the cusp of the Romantic period, writing about a Romantic subject, but in the Neoclassical style. Read about the Neoclassical and Romantic eras at the links below.

http://www.victorianweb.org/previctorian/nc/ncintro.html

https://excellence-in-literature.com/romantic-period-1820-1860-essayists-poets/

https://excellence-in-literature.com/the-romantic-era-by-steven-kreis/

This short article at The Victorian Web provides a helpful comparison between the Austen and the poet Percy Bysshe Shelley to illustrate the differences in style and emphasis between Neoclassical and Romantic eras.

http://www.victorianweb.org/previctorian/austen/nature.html

This very brief article offers a bit more insight into the literary periods and Austen's stance between them.

https://www.digitalausten.org/node/12

Places to Go

You may visit Chawton Cottage, the Hampshire home where Austen wrote some of her most beloved works. The website has a nice virtual tour.

https://janeaustens.house

If you'd like to visit some of the other sites from Austen's life and work, here is a virtual tour and some destination recommendations to get you started.

https://artsandculture.google.com/theme/10-virtual-tours-for-lovers-of-jane-austen/wALyslg9JF3OJA?hl=en

https://www.fodors.com/world/europe/england/experiences/news/5-essential-british-spots-for-jane-austen-fans-12229

Just for Fun

The Jane Austen Jokes page has several variations of a top ten song list, a hilarious list of Jane Austen punishments (things such as "An audience with the Queen accompanied by Mrs. Bennet" or "A tour of Rosings with Mr. Collins"), suggested answering machine messages, a money-making scheme from Mr. Wickham, and much more. This page is more than just fun; it will help you remember outstanding characteristics of each subject and give you ideas for the letters you will be writing for this module.

https://pemberley.com/janeinfo/austt10j.html

The Derbyshire Writers' Guild has created a site for stories written in the style of Jane Austen. Amazingly, there are over 2,400 stories on the site at this time. Perhaps you would like to contribute one as well? There are also message boards and links.

https://www.dwiggie.com

Assignment Schedule

Week 1

Begin reading the context resources and the focus text and follow the model in the Formats and Models chapter to write an Author Profile. Be sure to refer to your writer's handbook if you have questions about grammar, structure, or style.

Week 2

You will notice that the people of the Regency era wrote many letters. Assume the personality and language of one or more of the characters, and write three or four letters to/from another character. Consider not only the primary characters in the book but also supporting characters such as Mr. Collins, Mrs. Bennet, or Lady Catherine. Be sure to use the voice and style of each individual.

Week 3

Begin drafting a 750-word paper on one of the topics below. I recommend that you follow the writing process outlined in the "How to Write an Essay" chapter, consulting the models in the Formats and Models chapter and your writer's handbook as needed.

1- Model: Literary Analysis Essay and MLA Format Model

Prompt: *Pride and Prejudice* was originally titled *First Impressions*. Consider both titles in relationship to the characters of Elizabeth, Darcy, and Mr. Wickham, as well as in Austen's depiction of social class. What is the role of pride, prejudice, and first impressions in the development of relationships among these characters and in their social circles? What does Austen seem to suggest about pride, prejudice, and first impressions? Be sure to note Austen's use of irony, and provide specific textual support for your thesis.

2- Model: Poetry Analysis Essay and MLA Format Model

Prompt: Using one of the poems listed below, analyze the development of the setting and the significance of that development for the poem.

- William Wordsworth: "Tintern Abbey" or "Intimations"
- Samuel Taylor Coleridge: "Frost at Midnight" or "This Lime-Tree Bower My Prison"
- Percy Bysshe Shelley: "Ode to the West Wind" or "To a Sky-Lark"

- John Keats: "Ode on a Grecian Urn" or "To Autumn"

Turn in the draft at the end of the week, so your writing mentor can evaluate it using the Content standards (Ideas/Concepts and Organization) on the rubric.

Week 4

Use the feedback on the rubric along with the writing mentor's comments to revise your paper. Before turning in the final draft, be sure you have addressed any issues marked on the evaluation rubric, and verify that the thesis is clear and your essay is well-organized. Use your writer's handbook to check grammar or punctuation so that your essay will be free from mechanical errors. Turn in the essay at the end of the week so that the writing mentor can use the evaluation rubric in the "How to Evaluate" chapter to check your work.

Module 4.7

Great Expectations by Charles Dickens (1812–1870)

There are dark shadows on the earth, but its lights are stronger in the contrast.

—Charles Dickens

Focus Text

Great Expectations by Charles Dickens

Honors Texts

Oliver Twist or *David Copperfield* by Charles Dickens

Vanity Fair by William Makepeace Thackeray

Literary Period

Realist

Module Focus

You will observe the change from Romanticism to Realism in literature and art, and will develop an appreciation for Dickens' unforgettably vivid characterizations.

Introduction

During the reign of Queen Victoria, art and literature became increasingly focused on Realism, rather than an idealized Romantic picture of life. Rather than showing life as it could be under ideal circumstances, Charles Dickens, like many other Victorian writers, showed life as he believed it was. As a result, things can go seriously wrong in Dickens' world. His characters experience injustice, sorrow, and

Excellence in Literature: Reading and Writing through the Classics

pain, and they make choices for which there are real, logical consequences. Dickens draws upon his own life experience for some of these events, and his writings are credited with helping to bring about reformation of some of the social ills he observed.

Something to think about . . .

Pip learns many things over the course of the novel, and it seems that Dickens would have his readers understand these things as well. How do each of Dickens' main characters portray or respond to injustice, friendship, pride, ingratitude, love, faithfulness, suffering, and prejudice?

Be sure to notice . . .

Many of the characters in *Great Expectations* can be seen as pairs of opposites whose character or actions form a mirror image of the character or actions of the other. For example, Magwich and Miss Havisham are characters who experience a transformative event in life but choose to respond in very different ways. Estella and Biddy, and Joe and Pumblechook are other pairs of opposites. Why do you think that Dickens has created these contrasting characters? How does a mirror image sometimes help you see reality or truth more clearly?

Context Resources

Readings

Read the brief synopsis of the Realist period in the "Discerning Worldview Through Literary Periods" chapter of this book, as well as in the British Library article about literary Realism. This is important since it will help you recognize the ideas and worldview of this era.

https://www.bl.uk/romantics-and-victorians/articles/realism

The first line of George Orwell's article on Dickens begins, "Dickens is one of those writers who are well worth stealing." You'll have to read the article to find out what he meant, but it's well worth it. I suggest printing it out, as reading online isn't the best way to learn. Orwell writes well—two of his best-known works are *Animal Farm* and *1984*—so his comments are interesting and insightful.

https://orwell.ru/library/reviews/dickens/english/e_chd

Glencoe Literature Library offers a free, downloadable study guide that you may find helpful as you think through the novel. Don't get bogged down in filling in the blanks (unless you enjoy that sort of thing); just think about the various questions and points discussed.

http://www.glencoe.com/sec/literature/litlibrary/greatexpect.html

A Charles Dickens Journal offers a chronological overview of Dickens' books, plus a timeline of his life.

http://www.dickenslive.com

Here is a handy listing of Dickens 900+ characters. Dickens had a gift for naming his characters in a way that suggested something of their appearance or personality. Some of these names, such as Scrooge, are still commonly used as a metaphor for the character trait that Dickens ascribed to them, and others are just funny when you are reading the book aloud.

https://www.charlesdickenspage.com/charles-dickens-characters.html

The Author's Life

Look for *Charles Dickens,* G. K. Chesterton's short biography, at your library or online. Chesterton is a wonderful writer and a contemporary of C. S. Lewis and J. R. R. Tolkien. If you can't find the Chesterton biography at your library and don't want to read online, just read any brief biography your library offers.

https://www.chesterton.org/lecture-9/

https://amzn.to/3dWDLbZ

An outstanding page with a Dickens biography, maps of Dickens' London, glossary of characters, and much more. Be sure to visit all of it!

http://www.fidnet.com/~dap1955/dickens/

There are several very good sites that provide an overview of Dickens' life and other points of interest. The differing perspectives will help you gain a well-rounded view of Dickens and his novels.

http://www.victorianstation.com/authordickens.htm

http://tellingtrails.wordpress.com/2006/03/24/charles-dickens/

https://www.charlesdickenspage.com/index.html

https://www.charlesdickensinfo.com/life/

The Japan branch of the The Dickens Fellowship offers a family tree and the Dickens Family photo album.

http://www.dickens.jp/genealogy/genealogy-e.html

Spartacus shares a brief look at Dickens' life as a journalist, with a few interesting excerpts from his writing, including a report of a train accident, as well as an article written upon his death.

https://spartacus-educational.com/PRdickens.htm

Poetry

Read the discussion of Poetry of the Victorian Era at the site below.

https://www.poetryfoundation.org/collections/153447/
an-introduction-to-the-victorian-era

Elizabeth Barrett Browning

Read these selections from *Sonnets from the Portuguese* (#21, 22, 32, 43)

https://excellence-in-literature.com/elizabeth-barrett-browning-poetry/

Robert Browning

Notice that each of these poems tells a story, and that three of them are told in a conversational manner that reveals much of the narrator's personality. Browning is an engaging writer whose poetic narrators are as vividly memorable as Dickens' characters.

- "The Pied Piper of Hamelin: A Child's Story"
- "My Last Duchess"
- "Fra Lippo Lippi"

- "The Bishop Orders his Tomb at Saint Praxed's Church Rome, 15--"

https://excellence-in-literature.com/robert-browning-poetry/

Also read "How They Brought the Good News from Ghent to Aix."

https://excellence-in-literature.com/
how-they-brought-the-good-news-from-ghent-to-aix-by-robert-browning/

Audio

You should be able to find the audiobook of *Great Expectations* at your library or bookstore, or you can listen to a free amateur audio recording from Librivox:

http://amzn.to/2qdAiKh

https://librivox.org/great-expectations-by-charles-dickens/

Listen to this NPR audio interview of contemporary writer John Irving as he describes his first encounter with *Great Expectations* and Dickens' influence on his writing. The audio may pause occasionally as you listen, but it is interesting, insightful, and well worth hearing. Listen also to the other brief interview (listed on the same page) in which he discusses overcoming his own lack of talent through patient rewriting: "Irving on Overcoming His 'Lack of Talent' Through Rewriting." Revision is an important part of a writer's life, so do not miss this.

https://www.npr.org/templates/story/story.php?storyId=1905390

Music

In his work, Charles Dickens uses music to set scenes and define characters. Here's a look at some of the music he mentioned and what he enjoyed listening to.

https://www.wqxr.org/story/185550-too-busy-read-charles-dickens-try-music/

A free, downloadable audiobook called *Charles Dickens and Music* is available from Gutenberg.org.

http://www.gutenberg.org/etext/16595

Parlor or chamber music was popular during the Victorian era. Listen to the music of Franz Lizst, Felix Mendelssohn, and Frederic Chopin to hear the kind of music Dickens may have heard. Operas by Richard Wagner were also popular during this era. You may listen to these composers on any streaming service.

Video

You may enjoy the well-reviewed 1946 production of *Great Expectations*, which can most likely be obtained from your library. You can read more about this film version and watch a trailer at this link:

https://excellence-in-literature.com/great-expectations-1946-film

Here is an animated video biography of Charles Dickens. Don't miss this!

http://www.bbc.co.uk/drama/bleakhouse/animation.shtml

Turner Classic Movies has created a travel video of Dickens' London. If it is available at your library, it is worth seeing because it can help you to visualize Dickens' settings and see the appalling poverty that existed in this era.

https://shop.tcm.com/charles-dickens-london-works-charles-dickens-london-works/881482315994

Visual Arts

Illustrations from Dickens' novels

https://www.charlesdickenspage.com/charles-dickens-illustrations.html

Use an art history book to look up artists and techniques, such as lithography, from the Victorian era, especially the artists of the Barbizon School. Notice the common elements and themes in the paintings you see, and especially observe the ways in which style and subject matter changed from the beginning to the end of the nineteenth century. Be sure to note artists such as William Powell Frith, John Constable, and John Atkinson. This art is a visual counterpart to the changes that took place in literature, and seeing the connection will help you understand the Victorian/Realist worldview. You may view a few examples of Victorian-era art at the Metropolitan Museum of Art website and *The Victorian Web*.

https://www.metmuseum.org/toah/keywords/victorian-art/

http://www.victorianweb.org/art/index.html

Historical Context

Take a look at History.com's timeline of the Victorian era and the many events and changes that took place over the decades of Queen Victoria's reign.

https://www.history.com/topics/19th-century/victorian-era-timeline

Read "An Introduction to Victorian England" at the English Heritage site (first link) and "Social Life in Victorian England" (second link). Also read at least two topics from the British Library's Victorian Britain page (third link).

How would you feel about living in this place at this time in history?

https://www.english-heritage.org.uk/learn/story-of-england/victorian/

https://sites.udel.edu/britlitwiki/social-life-in-victorian-england/

https://www.bl.uk/victorian-britain

The *Charles Dickens Page* has an excellent map of Dickens' London. This can help you to orient yourself to the world in which Dickens lived and placed his characters

https://www.charlesdickenspage.com/charles-dickens-london-map.html

Places to Go

If you have a chance to go to London, take the Dickensian London walking tour outlined in this article in *The Christian Science Monitor*. As you read Dickens' works, you will notice that the city seems almost like another character in the novels. Dickens' descriptions are so vivid that when you see the streets where he walked, you will feel almost as if you have been there before.

https://www.csmonitor.com/2004/0128/p16s02-trgn.html

Richard Jones' website of *London Walking Tours* offers a detailed guide for a Dickens London walk, with background information on the sights to be seen.

https://www.london-walking-tours.co.uk/dickens_london_walk.htm

The creatively designed Charles Dickens Birthplace Museum in Portsmouth (UK) offers a Virtual Guide online tour and some interesting snippets of information.

https://charlesdickensbirthplace.co.uk

The Charles Dickens Museum in London is housed in Dickens' former home and offers "paintings, rare editions, manuscripts, original furniture, and many items relating to the life of one of the most popular and beloved personalities of the Victorian age."

https://dickensmuseum.com

Just for Fun

This article explores "Dickens' Genius for Comedy" with examples from *Great Expectations*. Even when Dickens is writing about difficult things, he can be quite funny, so it's helpful to understand and be able to spot his humor.

https://exec.typepad.com/greatexpectations/dickens-genius-for-comedy.html

Be sure to explore "The Dictionary of Victorian London," an entertaining website created by author Lee Jackson. Don't be put off by the odd front page—it's designed like the front cover of a book. Just click a title such as "The Cat's Meat Shop" (the blog) and you'll move into the site and be able to see "Mr. Jackson's Daguerreotypes" and other articles.

http://www.victorianlondon.org/lee/website.htm

The "Can You Survive Dickens' London?" game is no longer available, but here are a few other games you might enjoy.

https://www.charlesdickensinfo.com/games/

Assignment Schedule

Week 1

Begin reading the context resources and focus text. Follow the model in the Formats and Models chapter to write an Author Profile. Be sure to refer to your writer's handbook if you have questions about grammar, structure, or style.

As you read the novel, make a list of each character's full name, and note the personality trait, virtue, or vice that seems to exemplify the character. Which name seems to best portray the character's personality?

Week 2

Write a Historical Period/Event Approach Paper, following the format in the Formats and Models chapter, on the Industrial Revolution in England and its effect on the daily lives of London residents. In addition to the context links I have provided, you may use other resources such as your encyclopedia, the library, and quality Internet resources to complete this assignment.

Week 3

Begin drafting a 750-word paper on the topic below. I recommend that you follow the writing process outlined in the "How to Write an Essay" chapter, consulting the models in the Formats and Models chapter and your writer's handbook as needed.

Model: Literary Analysis Essay and MLA Format Model

Prompt: How do Pip's expectations, and his relationships with Joe, Estella, Magwitch, and Miss Havisham, affect his growth and development as a mature character? How do these relationships change over the course of the novel? Be sure to offer specific textual support for your thesis.

Week 4

Use the feedback on the rubric along with the writing mentor's comments to revise your paper. Before turning in the final draft, be sure you have addressed any issues marked on the evaluation rubric and verify that the thesis is clear and your essay is well-organized. Use your writer's handbook to check grammar or punctuation so that your essay will be free from mechanical errors. Turn in the essay at the end of the week so that the writing mentor can use the evaluation rubric in the "How to Evaluate" chapter to check your workk.

Module 4.8

Wuthering Heights by Emily Brontë (1818–1848)

Proud people breed sad sorrows for themselves.

—Emily Brontë

Focus Text

Wuthering Heights by Emily Brontë

Honors Texts

The Tenant of Wildfell Hall by Anne Brontë

Jane Eyre by Charlotte Brontë (if you did not read this in *Introduction to Literature*)

Frankenstein by Mary Shelley

Literary Period

Romantic/Realist

Module Focus

You will learn to recognize elements of the Gothic sub-genre of literature and will analyze the paired and circular elements of this intricately plotted novel.

Introduction

As you read about the lives of Emily Brontë and her family, you will discover a story that is almost stranger than fiction. Like the characters in *Wuthering Heights*, they lived a secluded life in a remote parsonage near the moors in England, and their lives seemed to be a series of unfortunate events. *Wuthering Heights* was not well received at its publication, and might have languished in obscurity without the later advocacy of poets Matthew Arnold and Algernon Swinburne, and author G. K. Chesterton. Emily Brontë died without knowing that Heathcliff and Catherine would go on to capture the imagination of readers for generations to come.

Something to think about . . .

The Brontë sisters were greatly influenced by their reading. In addition to the Bible, they had access to the works of Sir Walter Scott, Lord Byron, John Bunyan, and Samuel Johnson, among others. They also read Romantic poetry, Roman history, and fairy tales. Can you see how each type of literature helped to inspire or shape Emily Brontë's imagination and the type of story she chose to tell? Think about the type of literature you read. Can you see its influence in your writing?

Be sure to notice . . .

Although *Wuthering Heights* was published during the era of literary Realism, the setting and some of the plot elements belong much more strongly to the Romantic tradition. Watch for ideas that fit into each of these literary periods and read the poems recommended in the Poetry section to help you understand the author's perspective.

Context Resources

Readings

Professor Bridget M. Marshall offers an enlightening explanation of the differences and similarities in Gothic and Romantic literature.

Caden

http://faculty.uml.edu/bmarshall/romanticismandgothicartlit.html

It is important to recognize Romantic and Gothic elements that Emily Brontë incorporated into *Wuthering Heights*. In the two articles below, Dr. Lilia Melani of Brooklyn College identifies these elements and explains them in the context of *Wuthering Heights*.

Romantic: http://academic.brooklyn.cuny.edu/english/melani/novel_19c/wuthering/romantic.html

Gothic: http://academic.brooklyn.cuny.edu/english/melani/novel_19c/wuthering/gothic.html

Heathcliff is a larger-than-life literary character known as a Byronic hero. Learn what this means on Dr. Kip Wheeler's website for his students at Carson-Newman College.

http://web.cn.edu/kwheeler/lit_terms_B.html#byronic_hero_anchor

After you read *Wuthering Heights*, you may enjoy Jane Austen's *Northanger Abbey*, which is an amusing parody of some of the Gothic novels she had read. I recommend the Modern Library Classics paperback for its excellent introduction to the story.

Don't miss Charlotte Brontë's introduction to *Wuthering Heights*, "Biographical Notice of Ellis and Acton Bell." In this she explains why she, Emily, and Anne had initially published their works under a pseudonym, and touchingly relates the story of her sisters' brief lives. You will find this as part of many good editions of *Wuthering Heights*, or online.

https://excellence-in-literature.com/
charlotte-brontes-introduction-to-wuthering-heights/

The Author's Life

Look for Robert Barnard's *Emily Brontë*, part of the outstanding British Writer's Lives series, at your library or online. It's short and well-illustrated, and well worth reading.

https://amzn.to/2MQ6PHo

Professor Sara Selby of Waycross College (GA) has written an excellent short biography of Emily Brontë, with resources listed for further reading.

Amelia

https://excellence-in-literature.com/emily-bronte-a-biographical-sketch-by-sara-selby/

Other good resources you may find at your libary:

The Oxford Companion to the Brontës by Christine Alexander and Margaret Smith

The Brontës: A Life In Letters by Juliet Barker

Read this short biographical sketch of Emily Brontë by Professor Sara Selby of Waycross College (GA).

https://excellence-in-literature.com/excellence-in-lit/
emily-bronte-a-biographical-sketch-by-sara-selby

Haworth Village offers a wonderful Brontë site with biographies, photos of the parsonage, and more. Be sure to read at least three of Emily's poems here:

http://www.haworth-village.org.uk/brontes/bronte.asp

The Victorian Web, owned by a university professor, is a good source for information about Victorian authors. You may read about Emily Brontë and her works, as well as about the cultural context of *Wuthering Heights* and the themes and techniques that Brontë uses. This is not a pretty or flashy high-tech site, but the information is sound; do not hesitate to explore the rest of the site (click on "Home" at the top of the page or "The Victorian Web" at the bottom of the page) to learn more about this time period.

http://www.victorianweb.org/authors/bronte/ebronte/index.html

Poetry

Read about Victorian Poetry at the British Library.

https://www.bl.uk/romantics-and-victorians/themes/victorian-poetry

Read some of Emily Brontë's poetry at the sites below. Be sure to especially read "No coward soul is mine," the poem that American poet Emily Dickinson chose to have read at her own memorial service. This poem gives an entirely different impression of Brontë's worldview than does *Wuthering Heights*. Notice how vividly her imagery reflects her surroundings.

Addie

https://excellence-in-literature.com/no-coward-soul-is-mine-by-emily-bronte/

https://rpo.library.utoronto.ca/poets/brontë-emily-jane

http://academic.brooklyn.cuny.edu/english/melani/novel_19c/wuthering/poetry.html

George Gordon, Lord Byron, is thought to have greatly influenced Brontë's writing. Read the poems below and any others that interest you.

- "Prometheus"
- "She Walks in Beauty"
- "Darkness"

https://excellence-in-literature.com/poetry-by-george-gordon-lord-byron/

Samuel Taylor Coleridge was another writer who wrote in the Gothic tradition.

- "The Rime of the Ancient Mariner" or

- "Christabel"

  https://rpo.library.utoronto.ca/poets/coleridge-samuel-taylor

Audio

You may listen to the audiobook of *Wuthering Heights* at your library, online, or as a free amateur recording at Librivox.

  https://librivox.org/wuthering-heights-by-emily-bronte-2/

  https://amzn.to/3qhCrmD

Listen to "Music on Christmas Morning," an interesting poem by Anne Brontë.

  Samuel

  https://reelyredd.com/0307anne_bronte.htm

Music

Savannah

Some of Emily Brontë's poems have been set to music. You may see these, along with the composer's name, on the *The Lied and Art Song and Choral Texts Archive*. If you would like to hear the songs, there are links to sources for recordings.

  https://www.lieder.net/lieder/get_author_texts.html?AuthorId=383

Visit the links below to hear samples of music that the Brontë sisters most likely heard during their lifetime.

  http://akademisk.kor.dk/lyt-e.htm

Giuseppe Verdi

  https://www.classiccat.net/verdi_g/index.php

Felix Mendelssohn-Bartholdy

  https://www.classiccat.net/mendelssohn-bartholdy_f/index.php

Ludwig van Beethoven

  https://www.classiccat.net/beethoven_l_van/index.php

Video

The 1939 movie of *Wuthering Heights*, starring Laurence Olivier and Merle Oberon, is a well-done black-and-white classic. You may read commentary, see stills, and even watch the entire film online (with brief commercials).

Jacob

  https://excellence-in-literature.com/wuthering-heights-1939-movie-trailer/

  https://www.imdb.com/title/tt0032145/

Visual Arts

One of the most visible reminders of the Victorian period is the Gothic Revival architecture seen in many nineteenth-century buildings. This complex, highly ornamented style seems to be a visual counterpart to the elaborate structure of Victorian novels such as *Wuthering Heights*. Read about this movement and see examples in your art history book, encyclopedia, or online. The *Britain Express* site offers a good introduction to the style.

Caleb

https://www.britainexpress.com/architecture/gothic-revival.htm

Queen Victoria reigned for the last nineteen years of Emily Brontë's life, and a very long time overall (1837–1901) The world changed a great deal during her reign, and the art and literature that emerged during this period reflects this shift. Can you see some of the themes of Romanticism and the Gothic tradition in these examples?

https://excellence-in-literature.com/victorian-art/

Take this brief "Virtual Literary Tour of The Brontë Sisters" to see some of the places that inspired the sisters' work.

https://artsandculture.google.com/story/FwLyGtCo6USyJA

Historic Context

Some of the ideals of the Romantic period are evident in Emily Brontë's work

Griffin

https://excellence-in-literature.com/introduction-to-romanticism-from-lilia-melani/

Patrick Brontë, father of the Brontë sisters, was sponsored for ordination in the Church of England by famed reformer and anti-slavery activist, William Wilberforce and spent the remainder of his life in the ministry. To understand a bit more about Wilberforce and the political struggles during the Brontës' time, read the short Wilberforce biography (or *Hero for Humanity: A Biography of William Wilberforce* by Kevin Belmonte) below.

http://abolition.e2bn.org/people_24.html

"Walking the landscape of Wuthering Heights" offers a visual introduction to the Brontës' world.

https://www.bl.uk/romantics-and-victorians/articles/
walking-the-landscape-of-wuthering-heights

This rather odd timeline includes events from the Brontë sisters' lives along with events in photographic history.

https://brontesisters.co.uk/timeline.html

Places to Go

The Brontë Society actively preserves and promotes the work of the Brontë sisters, and offers events and activities at the Brontë Parsonage Museum in West Yorkshire, England. The webpage titled "Visiting" offers a brief video of the museum and its exhibits.

Emma

https://www.bronte.org.uk

https://www.yorkshire.com/places/west-yorkshire/bradford/haworth

Just for Fun

Here are ten little known facts about Emily Bronte—some are quite surprising!

Dayton

https://www.thehistorypress.co.uk/
articles/10-things-you-didn-t-know-about-emily-brontë/

Assignment Schedule

Week 1

Begin reading the context resources and focus text. Follow the model in the Formats and Models chapter to write an Author Profile. Be sure to refer to your writer's handbook if you have questions about grammar, structure, or style..

Week 2

Imagine that the characters in *Wuthering Heights* are your neighbors. Assume the role of a modern journalist, and write a feature story, set in the present time, about Hareton and Cathy's engagement, with an interesting summary of their troubled family history. Make it as long as necessary to tell a good story.

If you need extra help with feature article format, consult your writer's handbook or the article below.

https://excellence-in-literature.com/journalism-story-structure-by-mark-grabowski/

Week 3

Begin drafting a 750-word paper on one of the topics below. I recommend that you follow the writing process outlined in the "How to Write an Essay" chapter, consulting the models in the Formats and Models chapter and your writer's handbook as needed.

1- Model: Literary Analysis Essay and MLA Format Model

Prompt: In *Wuthering Heights*, Brontë works with many paired elements. Consider her intention and the effect of twos: Wuthering Heights and Thrushcross Grange; two families, each with two children; several marriage pairings; two primary narrators; and the doubling-up of names.

2- Model: Compare/Contrast Essay and MLA Format Model

Prompt: Consider how the final pairing of Hareton Earnshaw and Cathy Linton brings symmetry to the novel's structure and compares or contrasts with the previous pairings of their parents. Provide quotes from the text to support your thesis.

For additional help, use your writer's handbook or refer to the "How to Write a Compare/Contrast Essay" article at:

https://excellence-in-literature.com/resources-for-teaching/
how-to-write-a-compare-contrast-essay

Turn in the draft at the end of the week, so your writing mentor can evaluate it using the Content standards (Ideas/Concepts and Organization) on the rubric.

Week 4

Use the feedback on the rubric along with the writing mentor's comments to revise your paper. Before turning in the final draft, be sure you have addressed any issues marked on the evaluation rubric, and verify that the thesis is clear and your essay is well-organized. Use your writer's handbook to check grammar or punctuation so that your essay will be free from mechanical errors. Turn in the essay at the end of the week so that the writing mentor can use the evaluation rubric in the "How to Evaluate" chapter to check your work.

Module 4.9

To the Lighthouse by Virginia Woolf (1882–1941)

When the shriveled skin of the ordinary is stuffed out with meaning,
it satisfies the senses amazingly.

—Virginia Woolf

Focus Text

To the Lighthouse by Virginia Woolf

Honors Texts

Space Trilogy by C. S. Lewis

- *Out of the Silent Planet, Perelandra, That Hideous Strength*

Literary Period

Modernist

Module Focus

In this module you will observe a shift from order, direct representation, and harmony to randomness, impressionism, and dissonance, in art, poetry, music, and literature. Consider how this reflects the Modernist worldview.

Introduction

To the Lighthouse is a novel in which not much happens. Although it is divided into three parts—"The Window," "Time Passes," and "The Lighthouse"—it is difficult to think of the story in terms of the classic "exposition, climax, and conclusion" story arc. The narrative is presented in fragmentary scenes, with the perspective slipping from one character to another. You will view scenes from each character's eyes and be immersed in each individual's emotional responses. Woolf writes beautifully, and even though there is not a straightforward plot progression, you will finish with a sense of knowing at least a few of the characters fairly well, though in a misty, impressionistic way.

Something to think about . . .

Time is blurred in this novel. The first and longest section takes place over a single day; the second and briefest section, "Time Passes," covers about ten years; and the final section, "The Lighthouse," relates the events of a single morning. How does this affect your understanding of the book, and your feeling about the characters? Think back on events in your own life, and try to recall how time passed during significant events. Does Woolf accurately portray the way that people perceive time?

Be sure to notice . . .

The narrative techniques used in this novel are known as "stream-of-consciousness" and "free indirect discourse." While you may find that the lack of a plot makes it challenging to follow the structure of the book, you will need to think about why Woolf chooses to write her book this way. What do these new narrative techniques achieve that is not present in more structured novels? How do they influence your reading of the book and your understanding of the characters?

Context Resources

Readings

What is Modernism? Here is a brief introduction to this literary period and the factors that influenced its development. When you have read it, make a bulleted list of things that were done differently in the Modernist period than in previous literary periods.

https://kids.britannica.com/students/article/Modernism/341223

For a more in-depth look at why many of the changes in literature occurred, you may read an introduction to "Modernism, Modernity, & the Avant-Garde" in the online textbook posted at the link below.

https://mla.hcommons.org/deposits/objects/hc:25520/datastreams/CONTENT/content

University of Toronto professor Dr. Melba Cuddy-Keane offers a brief comparison of Victorian and Modernist literature. This is very helpful, so feel free to print it out for your notebook.

https://excellence-in-literature.com/victorian-modern-comparison/

Here is a study guide by Dr. Catherine Decker, an English professor. You do not need to answer all the questions, but they may help you make sense of the text:

https://excellence-in-literature.com/to-the-lighthouse-study-guide/

The Author's Life

Look for Ruth Webb's *Virginia Woolf*, part of the outstanding British Library Writers' Lives series. If you can't find, it, another middle-grade biography is acceptable. I don't recommend most adult biographies of Woolf.

This very brief biography of Virginia Woolf will give you an introductory overview of her life:

http://www.literaturecollection.com/a/virginia-woolf/

Poetry

T. S. (Thomas Stearns) Eliot (1888–1965)

- "The Hippopotamus"
- "The Love Song of J. Alfred Prufrock"
- "Journey of the Magi"
- "Four Quartets" (listen to T. S. Eliot read this at the link below)

  "Four Quartets" are four interlinked poetic meditations with the common theme being man's relationship with time, the universe, and the divine. Like Eliot's earlier poem, "The Waste Land," the "Four Quartets" seem to also reflect the ideas of the four elements (air, earth, water, and fire). In The New Poetic, Dr. S. K Stead suggests that each of the four poems has five movements, including

- The movement of time, in which brief moments of eternity are caught;
- Worldly experience, leading to dissatisfaction;
- Purgation in the world, divesting the soul of the love of created things;
- A lyric prayer for, or affirmation of the need of, intercession; and

- The problem of attaining artistic wholeness, which becomes an analogue for and merges into the problem of achieving spiritual health.

https://excellence-in-literature.com/t-s-eliot-poetry/

https://excellence-in-literature.com/hollow-men-four-quartets/

http://www.davidgorman.com/4quartets/

https://poetryarchive.org/poet/t-s-eliot/

Read the annotations for each of these poems (search for T.S. Eliot; then scroll to the correct poems):

http://rpo.library.utoronto.ca

W. H. (Wystan Hugh) Auden (1907–1973)

- "Musée des Beaux Arts"

This poem was inspired by the painting of *Landscape with the Fall of Icarus* by Pieter Bruegel the Elder that Auden saw in the Musée des Beaux Arts. A cropped version of this painting serves as the cover image of this book, but you can see the whole thing and read about the painting and the myth at the British Library.

https://www.bl.uk/collection-items/landscape-with-the-fall-of-icarus

William Butler Yeats (1865–1939)

- "The Second Coming"

https://excellence-in-literature.com/the-second-coming-by-william-butler-yeats/

Gerard Manley Hopkins (1844–1889)

Although Gerard Manley Hopkins (one of my favorite poets) lived during the Victorian era, he is considered by some to have been a pioneer of the Modernist style. At the very least, he strongly influenced Modernist poets such as T. S. Eliot and W. H. Auden. In order to understand how original his style was, listen to the poems as well as reading them.

- "God's Grandeur"
- "The Windhover"
- "Thou Art Indeed Just, Lord" (Justus Quidem tu es, Domine)

https://excellence-in-literature.com/gerard-manley-hopkins-poetry/

Richard Austin is an actor who specializes in reciting Hopkins' poetry from memory. If you ever have an opportunity to attend one of his live performances, do not miss it! Listening to Mr. Austin bring Hopkins' poetry alive is an unforgettable experience. He does an excellent job with the last poem mentioned above, which you can hear at this link:

https://excellence-in-literature.com/richard-austin-recites-hopkins-poetry/

Audio recordings of other poems by Hopkins, read by Walter Rufus Eagles:

http://www.eaglesweb.com/Sub_Pages/hopkins_poems.htm

Short Stories

The short story form showcases slightly different aspects of the Modernist style. Here are three examples to enjoy.

"Kew Gardens" by Virginia Woolf

https://excellence-in-literature.com/kew-gardens-by-virginia-woolf/

"The Other Side of the Hedge" by E. M. Forster

https://excellence-in-literature.com/the-other-side-of-the-hedge/

"The Reticence of Lady Anne by Saki" (H. H. Munro)

https://excellence-in-literature.com/the-reticence-of-lady-anne-by-saki/ OR

https://americanliterature.com/author/hh-munro-saki/short-story/the-reticence-of-lady-anne

Audio

Virginia Woolf's prose can be as beautiful as poetry, so it's worth listening to at least a little bit of the book. You can get the audiobook of *To the Lighthouse* at your library or online, where you can at least listen to a sample of the recording. If you listen to it as an audiobook, you will probably still need to read along because it can be easier to follow that way.

https://amzn.to/3kYqS2v

Listen to this delightful 1937 BBC recording of Virginia Woolf talking about words. Her love for words clearly comes through—be sure to notice her use of personification and metaphor. The second link offers the same recording as an animated video..

https://excellence-in-literature.com/virginia-woolf-radio-recording/

https://www.bbc.com/culture/
article/20160324-the-only-surviving-recording-of-virginia-woolf

NPR offers "Virginia Woolf, At Intersection Of Science And Art," and an except about her writing technique from the book *Proust Was A Neuroscientist* by Jonah Lehrer. This is quite interesting and should help you understand why she wrote in the style she chose.

https://www.npr.org/templates/story/story.php?storyId=93184407

Music

Igor Stravinsky's *The Rite of Spring* was a revolutionary work for its time. In fact, at its premiere, the audience rioted. View this interesting PBS video of this remarkable event, dramatically narrated by Michael Tilson Thomas, Director of the San Francisco Symphony.

http://www.pbs.org/keepingscore/stravinsky-rite-of-spring.html

At Professor Carol Reynold's blog, read Hank Reynolds' articles about Stravinsky's *Fireworks* and *Symphony of Psalms* and listen to the recordings on each page.

https://www.professorcarol.com/2015/01/16/fireworks-stravinsky/

https://www.professorcarol.com/2021/02/26/stravinsky-symphony-of-psalms/

Check out CDs from the library or listen online to music by Stravinsky and his contemporaries such as Benjamin Britten, Arnold Schoenberg, Charles-Camille Saint-Saëns (who stomped out of the premiere of *The Rite of Spring*, because he did not like the way Stravinsky used the bassoon), Béla Bartók, and Alban Berg. If you have listened to the other musical selections this year, the difference in structure and tone should be very apparent. Can you see how this is an auditory representation of the ideas that are behind the Modernist movement?

To listen online, go to an online streaming service such as Spotify and search for "Igor Stravinsky" to get started; you may also want to enter the names of the other composers listed above.

Video

There is a 1983 made-for-television drama of *To the Lighthouse* that may be available at the library. I have not seen this, so I cannot offer a recommendation. Please consult a reliable guide in order to decide whether it is suitable for your family.

https://www.imdb.com/title/tt0086452/

Visual Arts

Modern art reflects the same type of changes seen in Modernist literature and music. Read about Modern Art at My Modern Met at the first link; view some examples at the Tate Museum; then look at the sequence of paintings below, and observe how the subject and technique alters as Realism gives way to Impressionism, Post-Impressionism, and, finally, Cubism. Notice the dates and how quickly the changes took place and interestingly, how well the descriptions of Impressionism and Post-Impressionism fit Woolf's novel.

https://mymodernmet.com/what-is-modern-art-definition/

https://www.tate.org.uk/art/art-terms/m/modernism

Realism: William Bouguereau's (1825–1905) *The Knitting Girl* (1869)

https://www.k-state.edu/english/westmank/impressionism/bouguereau.htm

Paul Cezanne's Self-Portrait (1879)

https://www.k-state.edu/english/westmank/impressionism/cezanne_self-portrait.htm

Impressionism (sensory experience in a particular moment): Claude Monet's *Haystacks at Sunrise* (Snow Effect) (1890–1891)

https://www.k-state.edu/english/westmank/impressionism/monet.htm

Post-Impressionism (multiple perspectives in a single moment): Edouard Manet's *The Cafe Concert* (1878)

https://www.k-state.edu/english/westmank/impressionism/manet_cafe_concert.htm

Cubism: Pablo Picasso's *Le guitariste* (1910)

https://www.photo.rmn.fr/C.aspx?VP3=SearchResult&IID=2C6NU007DYZ8

Wassily Kandinsky (1866–1944)

https://www.tate.org.uk/art/artists/wassily-kandinsky-1382

Historic Context

Literature, art, and music are always influenced by the events of the time and place in which they are created. This article will help you understand why Woolf's writing, Stranvinsky's music, and Picasso's art all reflected something different from the art, music, and literature of earlier times.

https://www.irishtimes.com/culture/heritage/
out-of-the-wasteland-the-first-world-war-and-modernism-1.2190829

Virginia Woolf was part of a group of writers, artists, and thinkers known as the Bloomsbury Group. The Tate Museum offers an interesting online overview with many small illustrations of the group, its members, and its work. Read through this to help you understand Woolf's artistic influences and development. You can even take a quiz on the site if you are interested.

https://www.tate.org.uk/archivejourneys/bloomsburyhtml/

https://kids.britannica.com/students/article/Bloomsbury-group/317696

Places to Go

Charleston, the country home of the Bloomsbury Group, is located in Lewes East Sussex, and is open for tours.

https://www.charleston.org.uk/festival/

https://www.houseandgarden.co.uk/gallery/charleston

Monk's House, also in East Sussex, was Virginia and Leonard Woolf's home and is also open for tours.

https://www.nationaltrust.org.uk/monks-house?p=1356307088253

You can see Godrevy Lighthouse, the inspiration for the lighthouse in Woolf's tale, at the Cornwall website, and learn more about its history and how it works at the second link.

https://www.cornwalls.co.uk/cornwall/godrevy_lighthouse.htm

https://www.trinityhouse.co.uk/lighthouses-and-lightvessels/godrevy-lighthouse

Assignment Schedule

Week 1

Begin reading the context resources and focus text. Follow the model in the Formats and Models chapter to write an Author Profile. Be sure to refer to your writer's handbook if you have questions about grammar, structure, or style.

Week 2

Choose one of the following assignments to help you think through the novel.

1- Follow the instructions in the Formats and Models chapter to write an approach paper on *To the Lighthouse*.

2- Retell the three sections of the story in your own words. Do not just summarize, but create an enjoyable story of your own with enough detail to reveal the personalities of the characters and the mood of the original story. Make this as long as necessary in order to tell a good story.

Week 3

Begin drafting a 750-word paper on one of the topics below. I recommend that you follow the writing process outlined in the "How to Write an Essay" chapter, consulting the models in the Formats and Models chapter and your writer's handbook as needed.

1- Literary Analysis Essay and MLA Format Model

Prompt: In *To the Lighthouse*, what does the lighthouse and the journey to it seem to symbolize? Are these meanings consistent throughout the text, or do they shift, and if so how? What is the purpose of the journey, and what, if anything, does it accomplish? Remember to use quotes from the text to support your thesis.

1- Literary Analysis Essay and MLA Format Model

Prompt: The novel lingers on the creation of art and knowledge. How do different characters participate in creative acts, and how might we define art? Discuss the role of art in life, and use specific examples from the text to support your thesis.

Week 4

Use the feedback on the rubric along with the writing mentor's comments to revise your paper. Before turning in the final draft, be sure you have addressed any issues marked on the evaluation rubric, and verify that the thesis is clear and your essay is well-organized. Use your writer's handbook to check grammar or punctuation so that your essay will be free from mechanical errors. Turn in the essay at the end of the week so that the writing mentor can use the evaluation rubric in the "How to Evaluate" chapter to check your work.

Honors

Start writing, no matter what. The water does not flow until the faucet is turned on.

— Louis L'Amour

Key components of the Honors Option (in addition to regular assignments related to the focus text) include reading, writing, a final project, and an optional final exam.

- Reading: Usually one extra novel, play, or epic poem.
- Writing: An approach paper unless otherwise directed.
- Final project: One 6- to 10-page research paper (depending on student's grade level).
- CLEP test for some levels.

Extra Reading

Honors reading for each module is listed within the module. Each item has been chosen to coordinate in some way with the focus of the module. It might be an additional work by the focus text author or one of his/her contemporaries or something that is related in subject matter, theme, or genre.

Since the Honors option essentially doubles the reading load, you may need to think creatively about scheduling. You might finish the focus text during the first two weeks of the module and the Honors text in the last two weeks, or you might save a few of the texts to read as summer reading or between semesters.

Approach Papers

For one full-length honors text per module, you should complete an approach paper unless an alternative assignment is recommended. If more than one honors text is suggested with "AND" you would read both texts. If it's suggested with "OR", you may choose which to read and which to use as the subject for the approach paper. It is not necessary to write more than one honors approach paper per module.

Summary Titles

For each of the texts you read, create summary titles for each chapter or scene. A summary title is just what it sounds like—a title that summarized the contents or at least the main point of the chapter. This was common in the 18th and 19th centuries, as it gave potential readers a hint of what was coming. For novels that first appeared in serialized form, a summary title not only reminded readers of major characters and events in the story, it could also entice new readers to become interested. Here are some examples of summary titles from two of the books you will read in EIL.

From *Around the World in Eighty Days* by Jules Verne:

Chapter XI: In Which Phileas Fogg Secures a Curious Means of Conveyance at a Fabulous Price

Chapter XIV: In Which Phileas Fogg Descends The Whole Length Of The Beautiful Valley Of The Ganges Without Ever Thinking Of Seeing It

Chapter XXII: In Which Passepartout Finds Out That, Even At The Antipodes, It Is Convenient To Have Some Money In One's Pocket

From *Don Quixote* by Miguel de Cervantes:

Chapter VIII: Of The Good Fortune Which The Valiant Don Quixote Had In The Terrible And Undreamt-Of Adventure Of The Windmills, With Other Occurrences Worthy To Be Fitly Recorded

Chapter L Wherein Is Set Forth Who The Enchanters And Executioners Were Who Flogged The Duenna And Pinched Don Quixote, And Also What Befell The Page Who Carried The Letter To Teresa Panza, Sancho Panza's Wife

Like these examples, the summary titles you write should concisely summarize the contents of the chapter or scene in the most interesting way possible. Your summary titles can be helpful if you end up writing about the book in your research paper, but more importantly, these brief chapter or scene summaries will form a complete summary of the whole book and will help you remember what happened, including when, where, how, and why.

Research Paper Topic and Due Date

A research paper will be due two weeks after the end of the spring semester. The topic will be your choice of one of the authors you have studied this year. You can choose from the focus or Honors text authors, or even one of the poets that you read during the year. Your paper length will vary, depending on which EIL level you are in.

Format

— Length: E1–6 pages; E2–7 pages; E3–8 pages; E4–9 pages; E5–10 pages.

Your paper should be submitted in MLA format, the same format you have been using for essays. You will find more information about formatting in Section 9 (page 408) of the EIL *Handbook for Writers*, and at the OWL link below. Be sure to include a Works Cited page with a minimum of four resources. Up to two of the resources may be Internet sources chosen in accordance with accepted academic standards. You will find detailed, step-by-step instructions for researching, writing, and documenting your research paper at Purdue University's Online Writing Lab (OWL)

https://owl.purdue.edu/owl/general_writing/common_writing_assignments/ research_papers/index.html

Suggestions for the Author Research Paper

A research paper has been described as a thoughtful inquiry into a topic you find interesting. You will find detailed instructions in most writer's handbooks for how to do research, keep track of sources, list citations, format your research paper, and so forth. Once you have decided on the author who will be the focus of your Honors paper, here are things you may want to include:

- overview of the author's life;
- people, groups, and events that influenced the author's life and writing;
- overview of the author's body of work and his or her reputation among peers and in the general public;
- analysis of one or more of the author's best- or least-known works;
- how the author's work has influenced later writers or a genre of literature.

CLEP Test

If you have chose the Honors option, your final exam, which can be taken at the end of the school year, will be a CLEP test. Many colleges and universities grant advanced placement and/or college credit (up to six credits) for a passing score on these exams, so it is well worth the effort. (I earned forty-five credits toward my B.A. by taking exams on subjects I had studied on my own.)

These 90-minute, multiple-choice, computer-based exams can be taken by appointment at a local college or community college. Learn more about each exam, including what percentages of each exam are devoted to particular topics, and get practice materials at clep.collegeboard.org.

Suggested Schedule for CLEP Exams		
EIL Year	Suggested Exam	What it Covers
After E1, Introduction to Literature	Analyzing and Interpreting Literature* https://clep.collegeboard.org/ composition-and-literature/ analyzing-and-interpreting-literature	This skills-based exam focuses on questions about passages from American and British literature.
After E2, Literature and Composition	College Composition* https://clep.collegeboard.org/ composition-and-literature/ college-composition	This exam evaluates skills taught in most first-year college writing courses.
After E3, American Literature	American Literature https://clep.collegeboard.org/ composition-and-literature/ american-literature	This broad, general survey exam focuses on American literature from colonial time to the present.
After E4, British Literature	English Literature https://clep.collegeboard.org/ composition-and-literature/ english-literature	This broad, general survey exam focuses on major British authors and literary works.
After E5, World Literature	Humanities https://clep.collegeboard.org/ composition-and-literature/humanities	This exam evaluates knowledge of literature, art, and music and other performing arts.

*Option: The first two exams are skills-based exams, so you may wait to take them until you have done three or more years of EIL and other high school writing. The more practice you have, the better you are likely to score. The other three exams include knowledge-based questions, so it's best to take them right after the year of study is completed.

Tips for Writing a College-Ready Research Paper

You can find detailed instructions for planning and writing a research paper at Purdue University's Online Writing Lab and over 100 pages of instruction in the "Essays and Arguments" section in the Excellence in Literature *Handbook for Writers*, but what those instructions don't tell you is how to take your paper from snooze-worthy to spectacular. These seven tips will help you do it.

1: Know What is Expected

First, get acquainted with the assignment details. One of the best ways to do this is to copy the assignment into your brainstorming notebook and note any specific formatting requirements. Copying forces you to slow down and pay attention, and it can help you begin to discover resources and think through the topic.

2: Take Charge of Your Topic

Once you know what is expected, define your focus. It is both easier and more interesting to write in depth about a narrow topic than to offer a superficial look at a large topic. Here are two examples of how you might narrow the focus of a general topic.

History Example

General Subject: The French Revolution

Overall Focus: The general causes of the French Revolution

Narrow Focus: The social and political causes of the French Revolution

Narrower Focus: The immediate cause: the economic problem

Literature Example

General Subject: Hamlet by William Shakespeare

Overall Focus: Women in the play

Narrow Focus: A woman in the play: Ophelia

Narrower Focus: Ophelia's relationship with her father

Narrowest Focus: The scene in which Ophelia and Polonius first discuss Hamlet (Act I, Scene 3).

3: Start an Argument

A paper without an argument often sounds like a rewrite of a Wikipedia entry, so in order to take your paper to the next level, state an opinion in the thesis. This not only makes your paper more compelling, it also makes it easier to write. In the following example, consider the difference between a simple statement without an argument, and the more closely-focused thesis that provides a clear opinion to defend.

Statement: "Polonius is Ophelia's father, and when he dies, she goes insane."

Thesis with an argument: "Polonius's treatment of his daughter reveals a poisonous emotional climate at Elsinore, and suggests that his attitude and political ambitions are the source of much of the evil in the court."

Arguments belong in all types of research papers, including science and history. For example, if you are assigned a paper about Galileo, and you decide to focus on his astronomical observations, you wouldn't write an encyclopedia-style entry describing his work. For an outstanding paper, you might begin with an argument such as, "Galileo's astronomical observations were a breakthrough that effectively challenged the traditional views of the universe and introduced a bold new method of understanding the heavens." You could support this by offering evidence related to his observations, methods, and the traditional views challenged by his work. The strong, focused, argument-based thesis provides a foundation for everything that follows.

4: Craft an Orderly Introduction

The introduction of the paper will introduce your reader to the subject and focus of your paper, engage interest, and outline your thesis. The introduction to a spectacular research paper might follow the following model.

1. In the opening sentence, announce the general subject (piracy, a particular work of literature, a political event, a social issue, and so on). The general subject matter will often be contained in the essay topic your instructor has provided.

2. In the next two or three sentences, narrow the focus to one particular aspect of that general subject, so the reader understands that you are not dealing with all questions arising from that subject but only with one particular question or area of concern.

3. Finally in the last one or two sentences at the end of the introduction, define the thesis by announcing your opinion about that focus so that the reader understands what you are arguing.

5: Draw a Line of Evidence

Once the argument is introduced, establish a line of linked evidence that leads logically to the conclusion. Begin by brainstorming all the points you might want to discuss. Select evidence that most strongly supports the thesis, and write a topic sentence for each selected point. Topic sentences must argue only one piece of evidence, which will be supported in the balance of the paragraph. Create a topic sentence outline by arranging the topic sentences in the most persuasive order.

6: Make Every Paragraph Pull its Weight

In a spectacular research paper, every paragraph is made up of strong sentences that advance the argument in some way. Each paragraph should discuss one supporting point, and provide substantial evidence for that point alone. An excellent paragraph should include:

1. Topic sentence, an assertion announcing the main point of the paragraph, perhaps followed by one or two sentences reinforcing and clarifying the argumentative stance in this paragraph;

2. Evidence in the form of direct references to the text, quotations, statistics, summaries of relevant research data, and so on.

3. Interpretation of the evidence, a section which discusses in detail how the particular evidence you have introduced helps to back up the argumentative point announced in the topic sentence;

4. (Optional) Any qualifications you want to introduce to limit the argument, and especially to clarify the reliability of the evidence and thus the interpretations you have made of it;

5. Final summary point bringing the reader back to the point stressed in the topic sentence.

7: Wrap it Tightly

By the time you reach the end of your excellent research paper, the reader should have no doubt about the focus of the paper and the scope of your argument. Your concluding paragraph should wrap up your argument with a compelling summary of the evidence. If appropriate for your topic, you could also look ahead or suggest a course of action based upon the thesis.

As you work through your paper, read it aloud to yourself. Listen to see if sentences make sense and are gracefully linked. Once the final draft is complete, read it aloud to someone else and ask for feedback on its clarity, structure, and flow. Writing a strong research paper takes time, but with a focused topic, strong argument, and carefully organized and presented evidence, your paper can move to the head of the class.

Note: Examples adapted from the Excellence in Literature *Handbook for Writers*, available at Writers-Handbook.com.

Formats and Models

Read, read, read. Read everything—trash, classics, good and bad, and see how they do it.
Just like a carpenter who works as an apprentice and studies the master.
Read! You'll absorb it. Then write.
If it's good, you'll find out. If it's not, throw it out of the window..

— William Faulkner

There is a long and honorable tradition of using models or samples to learn to write well. The formats and models are you find here will help you understand the elements of each kind of assignment you will do. Each basic type of paper practiced in EIL is presented with a "Format"—instructions for what each paper should contain—plus a "Model"—a student-written sample of what a completed paper might look like. These models have been used with the permission of some of my former students and are examples of what each type of assignment should contain when it is turned in.

The final paper in this section is a general model of an essay written in MLA format with examples of how to integrate and format quotations of prose or poetry. This model will be useful for all your Week 3 writing assignments.

In every assignment, please use MLA format (see the final model in this section, titled "MLA Format Model"). Remember to put your name, the date, the class name, and the module number and focus text title in the top left corner of each assignment you turn in. For essays or stories, also copy the assignment prompt just below this information so that you will have it handy as you are writing, and your evaluator will know exactly what question you are answering.

Note to Parents About the Model Papers

When you look at these papers, please do not panic. They are the work of some of my best students over the years, and they offer a look at what is possible, not necessarily what is routinely expected. Also, please do not assume that a student's interpretation in the sample paper is the "right" one. It is simply that student's impression. Your student's paper may be quite different, and that is perfectly fine as long as his or her opinions are backed up by evidence (quotes) from the text. As for writing quality, if your student is not yet producing work of this caliber, be patient. With each completed assignment you will see growth and improvement, and that incremental growth is what you will build on. You don't have to start at the top to have good results; you just need to climb steadily!

∽

Approach Paper Format

One of my favorite tools for literary analysis is the approach paper. Although "approach paper" may seem to be an odd name for an analytical assignment, it makes sense when you realize that the exercise of writing each section of the approach paper helps to guide your thinking as you approach the essay assignment.

An approach paper consists of several sections:

I. **MLA-style heading** with your name, date, class, and name of the work you will be analyzing. (See sample for proper format.)

II. **Summary Paragraph:** A three- or four-sentence paragraph that summarizes the book or other work in as much descriptive detail as possible. Each of the sentences in your summary must begin in a different way, and sentences should be varied in length and full of interesting detail. If you need help with this, the *Handbook for Writers* provides guidance in how to form and style sentences and paragraphs, plus guidance for issues of grammar, style and usage. The summary is sometimes the most difficult section of the approach paper to write because it takes time to condense the events of a whole novel, play, or epic poem into just a few well-written sentences.

III. **Character Descriptions**: Choose and list three or four main characters in the work you are studying. In just four or five adjectives, vividly describe the character. This might be a good time to use some of the new or unusual vocabulary words you've encountered in the book, or to check the dictionary and thesaurus for ideas. Descriptive words may be used only once per approach paper, so if you use a word to describe one character, you may not use the same word to describe another character.

IV. **Discussion/Essay Questions**: Write three questions about the novel, poem, play, or essay. These questions should be thought-provoking and will almost always take more than one line to type because they ask readers to combine more than one idea. They must not be questions of fact, but of interpretation, just like the questions that are provided for your essay assignments. The act of writing this type of question helps you to think more insightfully about the characters in relationship to one another and to the setting, the author's style and intention, and the voice and reliability of the narrator. When you think seriously about these issues, you begin to approach an understanding of the text.

V. **Key Passage**: Choose the passage you feel is the most important passage in the work. This may be a brief paragraph, or it may be an entire page or more. Type it up word-for-word in the approach paper. Be sure to identify the speakers if the passage includes dialogue.

VI. **Key Passage Explanation**: In a fully developed paragraph, explain why your chosen passage is important to understanding the focus text. In your explanation make sure you integrate quotes (actual words or phrases) from the key passage to strengthen your explanation, using proper MLA format as demonstrated in your handbook or in the sample essay in this guide. Often, your chosen key passage will offer clues to the novel, poem, or play's themes. If you notice this, be sure to mention it in your explanation.

Approach Paper Model

Student's Name

Date

English V: Instructor's Name

Don Quixote Approach Paper

Summary:

Don Quixote by Miguel de Cervantes is the classic tale of a Spanish madman named Don Quixote, who decides to become a knight. Along with his devoted squire Sancho Panza, Don Quixote forces himself and others into undesirable adventures throughout the Spanish nation of Castille. But Don Quixote also finds that the world does not desire a return to the old world of chivalry, for he is scorned at every turn for his desire to revive a long-lost golden age of Europe. On two different occasions, in fact, a bachelor named Sansón Carrasco (disguised as a knight-errant) tries to defeat the deluded knight in jousts, attempting to order him to return to his hometown in La Mancha. On the second attempt, Sansón defeats Don Quixote, and grants him life under the condition that he return to his home and forsake the order of knight-errantry. After Don Quixote returns home, he regains his sanity and declares, "I now abhor all profane stories of knight-errantry."

Characters

- Sancho Panza: gullible, subservient, opportunistic, acquisitive
- Don Quixote: quixotic*, idealistic, chimerical, fatuous, psychotic
- Sansón Carrasco: covetous, arrogant, avaricious, pugnacious

Discussion Questions

- The characters in *Don Quixote* make numerous references to Miguel de Cervantes himself, as though the author were a contemporary of the characters. How is the author's opinion about himself portrayed in the book? What attributes of Cervantes' own life and philosophy are expressed within the characters?

- Much of the parody in *Don Quixote* is affected by the unusual combination between knight-errantry and sixteenth-century life. How do the civilizations of Amadis of Gaul and King Arthur of England differ from Don Quixote's world?

- Cervantes makes many references to the relationship between Moors and Christians in sixteenth-century Spain. Has the relationship changed since the age when the Moors were driven out of Spain? If so, how?

Key Passage, from Chapter XV of Book II, p. 627

In his first joust with Sansón Carrasco, Don Quixote emerges victorious from battle and elated with joy over his triumph. Afterward, the following passage ensues:

> Carrasco undertook the task [to defeat Don Quixote in a joust], and Tomé Cecial, Sancho's comrade and neighbor, a merry, scatterbrained fellow, offered his services as squire. Sansón armed himself as has been described and Tomé Cecial, to avoid being recognized by his comrade when they met, fitted on over his natural nose the false one already mentioned. And so they followed the same road as Don Quixote and very nearly reached him in time to be present at the adventure of the cart of Death, and at last they met in the wood, where everything that the extraordinary fancies of Don Quixote, who took it into his head that the bachelor was not the bachelor, Master Bachelor licentiate, because he did not find nests where he expected to find birds. Tomé Cecial, seeing how badly their plans had turned out and what a wretched end their expedition had come to, said to the bachelor: "For sure, Master Sansón Carrasco, we've met with our deserts. It is easy to plan and start an enterprise, but most times it is hard to get out of it safe and sound. Don Quixote is mad, and we are sane, but he comes off safe and in high spirits, while you, master, are left drubbed and downcast. Tell us, now, who is the greater madman, he who is so because he cannot help it, or he who is so of his own free will?"

Key Passage Explanation:

This passage offers a panoramic view of the whole paradox of Don Quixote. Don Quixote is mad, but the sane madness of his opponents is even worse, for in their depravity they are mad of their "own free will." We see in this passage that everyone is a sort of villain in this book. Don Quixote meets with his own hardships, but as Tomé Cecial points out, "We've met with our own deserts [deserved punishments]." Cervantes does not advocate the false chivalry promulgated in the books of knight-errantry, but neither does he support its alternative. By ridiculing both extremes, Cervantes tacitly expresses his desire for a balance.

Historical Approach Paper Format

Event or Era

Place

Time

Event Summary

Write an interesting one-paragraph summary of the period or event.

Key Players

Choose 3–4 key people involved in the event, and list 4–5 vividly descriptive words for each person. Words may not be used to describe more than one character.

Discussion Questions

Think carefully about the event, and write three analytical discussion questions.

Turning Point

Choose an event that seems to mark a significant turning point or climax in the period or event, and write a one-paragraph description.

Turning Point Explanation

Why do you believe this was a significant turning point? What happened afterward? Write a fully developed paragraph explaining your choice. Support your argument with quotes from the text or other sources, if appropriate.

〜

Historical Approach Paper Model

Student's Name

Date

English I: Instructor's Name

Event: Russian Revolution

Place: Russia

Time: 1917

Event/Era Summary

The Russian Revolution was not a single event in which Tsar Nicholas II was defeated and removed from power, but a broad expression of two events, the February

Revolution and the October Revolution. Leading up to the February Revolution, Russia experienced turmoil and political conflict over issues such as the country's economic condition and its prevailing failure in World War I. Conditions in Russia continued to worsen until a festival in one of Russia's prominent cities turned into a large protest, inducing Nicholas II to order a military intervention which proved futile, as much of his military was no longer loyal. This event caused Nicholas II to resign the position of tsar to his brother, Michael Alexandrovich, who was not willing to serve without election. Without anyone to fill the position, Russia had no other choice than to set up a temporary government, eventually headed by Alexander Kerensky. Another important character, Vladimir Lenin, plays a significant role in the October Revolution as a member of the communist revolution with a plan to overthrow the current government. Lenin's plan worked to perfection as military guards laid down their arms immediately without resistance. Alexander Kerensky soon fled the palace and the new government, led by Lenin, took effect.

Key Players

- Tsar Nicholas II: obstinate, neglectful, destructive, intelligent
- Vladimir Lenin: persuasive, radical, visionary, rebellious
- Alexander Kerensky: popular, successful, convincing, renowned

Discussion Questions

I.   Though it may have been due to his lack of political education, Nicholas II made many mistakes as a leader. What measures could he have taken in an attempt to avoid the widespread upheaval that occurred?

II. Why was Vladimir Lenin so successful in spreading the principles of Marxism? Did the people find hope in his ideas when it seemed as if there was no hope?

III. How did conditions change in Russia after the Revolution of 1917? In what ways did relations with other countries change?

Turning Point

Forced by the growing pressure to turn the economic momentum around and by overall unpopularity, Tsar Nicholas II stepped out of office. He gave his leadership role to his younger brother; however, he would not accept it without the vote of the people. Out of necessity the Russian Provisional Government was assembled in Petrograd to form some type of leadership.

The time of the resignation of Tsar Nicholas II is the first radical change of the Russian Revolution, but it also marks the end of tsarist rule in Russia. This created a need for a political change to sustain the government, leading into the Russian Provisional Government. Although this occurred during the February Revolution, these events allowed the happenings of the October Revolution to take place, thus completing the entire Revolution of 1917. This time period is a turning point because it started the transformation and provided an outlet for the following events to occur. Without these events it would have been extremely difficult for Lenin and his followers to procure leadership.

Author Profile Format

For each focus work it is important to complete an Author Profile. If you cannot find the recommended biography in your local library, feel free to substitute any short biography that you find. I suggest using biographies found in the middle-grade or young adult sections of the library, as they usually provide an adequate introduction to the author's life without dwelling unnecessarily on the less savory bits.

Name (including pseudonyms if any)

| **Birth Date** | **Place** |
| **Death Date** | **Place** |

Best-Known Works

Include three or more of the author's best or best-known works.

Brief Biography

- How does this author use his or her personal experiences in his or her work?
- What current events or public figures affected the author's life and writing?
- How do the places in the author's life show up in his or her writing?

Author Profile Model

Name: Washington Irving (pseudonyms include Dietrich Knickerbocker, Jonathan Oldstyle, and Geoffrey Crayon)

Birth Date: April 3, 1783 **Place:** Manhattan, NYC, NY

Death Date: November 28, 1859 **Place:** Sunnyside, Irvington, NY

Best-Known Works

- *The Legend of Sleepy Hollow, Rip Van Winkle, The Sketchbook of Geoffrey Crayon, The Life of George Washington, Knickerbocker's History of New York*

Brief Biography

Washington Irving used his experiences living in both Europe and America to write humorous and meditative stories popular in both the new and old worlds. Irving's life and work were influenced by the events of the Revolutionary War and the War of 1812, and he was also profoundly influenced by other writers (both European and American) of his time. His favorite childhood stories involved voyages to far-off lands. The places of Irving's life show up extensively in his writing. He wrote of England, America, and even lived in Tarrytown, New York, where he set *The Legend of Sleepy Hollow.*

Literature Summary Format

Novel or Story Title: Write the story's full title and subtitle, if any, here.

Author: Write the author's full name and pseudonym, if any.

Theme: What is the main idea that the author wants to convey? The theme is the big idea illustrated by the story's plot and characters. This can often be expressed in a proverb or phrase such as "honesty is the best policy" or "love never fails."

Characterization: WHO is the story about, and what are they like? How does the author show you this?

Plot: WHAT happens in the story?

Setting: WHEN and WHERE does the story take place?

Style: HOW does the author create a mood and tell the story?

Literature Summary Model

Novel or Story Title: "The Secret Life of Walter Mitty"

Author: James Thurber

Theme

"The Secret Life of Walter Mitty" explores the desire of every human being to be smarter, braver, and more important, and what happens when this fantasy world becomes an addiction more real than reality itself.

Characterization

Walter Mitty is humanity taken to an extreme. He is a daydreamer, imagining he is a Navy pilot flying through the most devastating hurricane in history when he is just driving his wife to her hair appointment, or envisioning himself as a world-renowned surgeon when he drives past a hospital. You also get the feeling that Walter may be aging and not "all there."

Plot

"The Secret Life of Walter Mitty" chronicles a day in Mitty's life and his struggles to complete his daily routine instead of slipping into his fantasy world.

Setting

The setting of 1940s England has very little effect on the story, except that certain buildings Mitty passes do occasionally prompt certain daydreams.

Style

The story is handled with a rather straightforward, simple style that changes for each daydream. For example, when he imagines himself as a combat pilot, the characters speak with an efficient, clipped style, using only as many words as are necessary.

Literary Analysis Model

The format instructions for this model are found in the chapters on "How to Read a Book" and "How to Write an Essay." You will find this model helpful for most of the essays assigned throughout the curriculum. Additional models for specific types of essays can be found in the Excellence in Literature *Handbook for Writers*.

Student Name

Date

Class Name

Module # and Focus Text Title

Prompt

Pride and Prejudice was originally titled *First Impressions*. Consider both titles in relation to the characters of Elizabeth, Darcy, and Mr. Wickham, as well as to Austen's depiction of social class. What are the roles of pride, prejudice, and first impressions in the development of relationships among these characters and their social circles? What does Austen seem to suggest about pride, prejudice, and first impressions? Be sure to note Austen's use of irony, and provide specific textual support for your thesis.

The Defects of Human Nature

Life in the early 1800s revolved primarily around the social aspects of life. Social conventions ruled the actions of young ladies and their mothers, guided their brothers in selecting a spouse, and even dictated with whom their families were permitted to associate. Jane Austen gently ridicules the rigid structure of her society's rules and regimens in her novel *Pride and Prejudice*. Through her ironic situations and comical views of life, she attempts to reveal some of society's faults and offer alternatives for the faulty tendencies of human nature.

Pride was an integral part of the nineteenth-century culture. At the very foundation of the separations between social classes, pride enabled entire families to choose not to associate with each other so as not to damage their own social reputations. Mr. Darcy, "a fine figure of a man" with "ten thousand [pounds] a year" (16), embodied this pride admirably. During the first ball he attended in Hertfordshire, his air of superiority proved that he was assuredly aware that his fortune was much larger than anyone's in the room and that his social status was accordingly higher. His reclusive nature and manners also added to the aura of pride which enveloped him.

Although his neighbors were gentlemen and gentlemen's daughters, Mr. Darcy believed that his income and social standing in London set him above the residents of Hertfordshire. Indeed, later he acknowledged that his parents "almost taught [him] to be selfish and overbearing—to care for none beyond [his] own family circle, to think meanly of all the rest of the world, to wish at least to think meanly of their sense and worth compared with [his] own" (274).

Mr. Darcy further displayed the pride which was so deeply ingrained in him when he bungled his first proposal to Elizabeth Bennet. Although he began acceptably with expressions of his love, "he was not more eloquent on the subject of tenderness than of pride" (149). The descriptions of his admiration soon turned to illustrations of the obstacles he overcame to stand before her and propose. Despite his intended purpose to depict the depth of his emotion, his expressions of "his sense of her inferiority … of the family obstacles which judgment had always opposed to inclination" (149) only served to anger and insult Elizabeth. Mr. Darcy's pride prevented him from understanding that the differences in social standing were evident to Elizabeth and that she would not be flattered by his explanations.

Although Elizabeth was not proud in the same manner as Mr. Darcy, she was not immune to human faults. Elizabeth's flaw was expressed in the more socially acceptable form of prejudice. Elizabeth discovered the danger of relying on first impressions as her relationships with Mr. Darcy developed. Mr. Darcy's actions at their first meeting prompted her to accept her community's harsh opinion of him as her own. Without making the effort to get to know Mr. Darcy, Elizabeth fixed her own views about his character and held "no very cordial feelings towards him" (17).

Elizabeth then repeated her mistake of allowing her impressions to turn into prejudice when she met Mr. Wickham. "… Struck with [Mr. Wickham's] air" (63) she formed her acquaintance with an inclination to approve of his actions. This inclination caused her to believe Mr. Wickham explicitly when he fabricated tales about Mr. Darcy. It reached to the extent that her friend felt the need to advise her not to "allow her fancy for Wickham to make her appear unpleasant in the eyes of a man of ten times his consequence" (77).

Ironically, Elizabeth did not begin to alter her prejudices until she accused Mr. Darcy of causing Mr. Wickham's "misfortune" (150). Mr. Darcy's account of the matters forced her to reverse her opinions about him and Mr. Wickham. "Every lingering struggle in [Mr. Wickham's] favor grew fainter and fainter" (161) as she recognized his indecent behavior and consequently scolded herself for not identifying them sooner. This discovery of the true character of these gentlemen was humiliating to Elizabeth as she had "prided [herself] on [her] discernment" (162). However painful this lesson may have been, Elizabeth benefited from it by gaining insight into the hazards of prejudice.

Although Jane Austen first titled her novel *First Impressions*, her final choice of *Pride and Prejudice* seems to fit her analysis of human behavior more suitably. Her humorous novel prodded her contemporaries to formulate their own opinions and not to rely on society's poor abilities or their own preconceived notions about themselves. It forced their descendants to confront their own human nature and face their personal defects.

⌒

Sample Compare/Contrast Essay Model

(*NOTE: This model contains spoilers for stories in Module 4.1, so you may want to read the stories before studying this example.*)

Student Name

Date

Class Name

Module # and Focus Text Title

Prompt: Choose two of the assigned stories, and write an essay comparing and contrasting ways in which the selected works are similar/different in one or two of the following areas: plot, theme, characterization, setting, and style.

Distinct Works of Art

"The Necklace" and "The Ransom of Red Chief" are two very different stories, and yet, when they are examined closely, a resemblance can be seen between them. The authors chose different ways to approach the stories, and very different character roles, but both produced well-written stories that captivate the reader's mind.

In "The Necklace," the plot is simple but interesting. The main character, Mathilde Loisel, receives an invitation to a party at the palace of Ministry, but is distressed by her lack of clothes and jewels to wear for the event. She buys a dress, and borrows a diamond necklace from Mme Forester. After the party, the necklace is nowhere to be found, but she can not bring herself to confess what had happened to Mme. Forester. Instead, she buys a necklace exactly like the one lent to her, which takes her ten years to pay for. During a friendly conversation with Mme. Forester years later, she discovers that the diamonds in the borrowed necklace were false.

The "Ransom of Red Chief" is created in a similar manner, with the story ending differently than the characters anticipated. In this rather amusing story, Bill and Sam kidnap a little boy Johnny, planning to ask money for the boy's return. The kidnappers thought that Johnny would be traumatized, and that Johnny's father, Ebenezer Dorest would be outraged by the boy's disappearance, but they were not. While being held hostage, Johnny entertains himself in the woods, playing Indians and Black Scouts with Bill and Sam. During the child's play, the men have some rather horrifying experiences while posing as Johnny's "Indian captives." They write to Mr. Dorset, demanding $1,500 for the boy's return as planned. In his reply, Mr. Dorset tells them that he will not pay the ransom, but will take Johnny off their hands for $250. Bill and Sam, aggravated by the little boy, pay the $250.

The plot itself is extremely different from The Necklace, but the story has similar results. In both cases, the characters did something that they knew was wrong, and in the end, rather than gaining something, they paid the consequences for their dishonesty or crime. Mathide Loisel would still have had to replace Mme. Forester's necklace, but would only have had the expense of false diamonds. In the Bill and Sam's case, if they had been truthful about their wrongdoing, it would have saved them the cost of bringing Johnny home.

Style is another focus in the stories. In The Necklace, the author uses dignified sounding words, which make graceful paragraphs throughout the story. It is written with such skill and craftsmanship that the reader is held in suspense until the end of the last paragraph. The very opposite of this writing style is found in The Ransom of Red Chief. Instead of using what might be thought of as "normal" speech, the characters use slang, and use imperfect grammar. Unlike The Necklace, it is an energetic and comical story that makes any reader twitch with even a slight smile.

These stories are both fabulous works of art, in which the characters learned valuable lessons. Although we may never be in a situation like the characters in the story, we can learn from them and apply the principles to our own lives.

&

Sample Poetry Analysis Model

Student Name

Date

Class Name

Module # and Focus Text Title

Prompt: Make a close reading of "God's Grandeur" or "The Windhover" by Gerard Manley Hopkins. Make sure you show how the images and figurative language in the poem complement one another. Show also how he uses sound, including consonance, assonance, and rhyme in constructing his poetic argument. Consider also how he develops his poetic argument from the beginning to the end of his poem.

Inspired by a Falcon

In "The Windhover," Gerard Manley Hopkins talks about watching a kestrel, a small falcon which hovers in the air. Dedicated to Christ, this poem celebrates the majesty, beauty, and power of one of God's creations. Hopkins describes the kestrel's flight, hovering, and dive, as well as his reaction to this display of strength. He is clearly awed, for "[his] heart …Stirred for a bird" (7–8).

Hopkins uses figurative language and imagery throughout "The Windhover." The title itself conveys the image of the kestrel hovering in the wind. In addition, the sounds of the poem correspond with its action.

In the first stanza Hopkins describes the kestrel's steady flying and gliding, as well as the poet's own admiration. The poem begins with "I caught this morning morning's minion, king- / dom of daylight's dauphin, dapple-dawn-drawn Falcon," (1–2).

The word "caught" is used figuratively, as in seen. The word "minion" means darling, and "Dauphin" is the title for the prince who is the heir to the French throne; Hopkins is acknowledging that the kestrel is the darling and ruler of the daylight. He admires "the achieve of, the mastery of the thing!" (7–8), as the kestrel flies uninhibited, master of flying and the air. Hopkins's use of the words "riding" (2) and "striding" (3) help us to see the image of the kestrel flying through the air. In addition, these words give us a sense of the kestrel moving smoothly with a sense of rhythm, which meshes well with his later image of skating. The kestrel glides or hovers through the air, just "As a skate's heel sweeps smooth on a bow-bend" (6).

This stanza has a rhythm that swings along, heightened by alliteration, assonance, and consonance, as in "dapple-dawn-drawn[.]" Later in the stanza Hopkins uses alliteration again to produce a smooth sound that imitates gliding. In addition, the way every line rhymes (they all end with "-ing") also emphasizes rhythm.

In the next stanza Hopkins is talking about the kestrel flying up and then diving down. He uses figurative language to convey the action. "Brute beauty and valour and act, oh, air, pride, plume, here / Buckle! AND the fire that breaks from thee"

(9–10). Hopkins describes the kestrel by its attributes, and the combined effect is an impression of soaring and climbing. The bird is not "valour and act … air, pride, plume," but it and its flight embody those ideas. "Buckle!" and its possible meanings are a one-word summary of what is happening: to get ready, to make fast, to fall through. The poem builds up speed and dives with the windhover. Hopkins uses lots of different consonants and vowels to create a jumbled sound of words climbing upon one another, building up to "Buckle!" just as the kestrel climbs up and then dives. The "fire that breaks from [the kestrel]" refers to the way the kestrel's wings flash open, revealing a reddish-brown color, as the bird nears the ground. Later in the stanza Hopkins refers to the windhover as a "chevalier" (11), which conveys the idea of nobility and strength and "valour" (9). A knight gallops across the countryside; the kestrel hovers and dives in the sky.

In the last stanza the poem flies swiftly and easily to the ground with the bird. This stanza is more quiet; Hopkins uses soft-sounding vowels and consonants. "Sheer plod make plough down sillion / Shine" (12–13) has smooth consonants that move steadily forward just like a plow. Hopkins compares this to the way the kestrel plows through the air. Matching with the earlier figurative language of fire, Hopkins presents an image of "blue-bleak embers, ah my dear, [that] / Fall, gall themselves, and gash gold-vermilion." The embers are falling, opening, and glowing. This helps us to see the image of the kestrel diving through the sky and flashing open his reddish-brown wings when he nears the ground, just as the embers "gash gold-vermilion." In the last line, "Fall, gall themselves, and gash gold-vermilion" (14), even though the g's are hard, the vowel sounds; particularly the use of ah (definitely an example of assonance), soften the line.

Throughout "The Windhover," Hopkins's awe is evident in his enthusiastic description. He conveys his message with words and sounds that echo and emphasize his story, making it a poem of both visual images and oral expression. He uses this method to involve and engage the reader in his experience. Hopkins's soaring poetry shares his awe of the kestrel and its Creator with the reader.

MLA Format Model

Use these format guidelines for all of your Week 3/4 assignments.

Your Name

Date

Class Name

Module # and Focus Text Title

For an EIL essay, please add the writing prompt at this point.

Making Your Essay Look Good:

The Basics of MLA Format

In the upper right-hand corner of each page, beginning with page two if you prefer, one-half inch from the top (the text of your essay should begin one inch from the top), place a header with your last name, a space, and the page number. In most word-processing programs, you can do this from the "View" menu by selecting "Header and Footer." [NOTE: This is not shown in these models, but should be done in your own essays.] You should have one-inch margins on the right, the left, and the bottom of your page, and your essay should be double-spaced (set line spacing in your word processing program—do *not* place a hard return at the end of each line). Use one space at the end of terminal punctuation.

When you quote poetry, if the quotation is three or fewer lines, fit it right into your text. For instance, if I want to let you know that Blake begins "The Ecchoing Green" by juxtaposing "merry bells [that] ring / To welcome the spring" and "The sky-lark and thrush, / The birds of the bush," I would do it like I just did it. I might also note that Blake emphasizes this juxtaposition by the rhyme of "ring" and "sing," a rhyme that helps connect the natural and the human worlds because the sound describing the voices of the birds in the green echoes the sound describing the voice of human-made bells.

Notice that I keep the punctuation and the upper-case letters as they are in the poem. If I want to add something to make the quotation fit the grammar of my sentence, I do so by indicating the addition with brackets. If I wanted to leave something out of the poem and pick up the quotation a few words later, I would use ellipses, which are three dots with spaces between them (. . .).

I might then want to point out that, while "Old John" chimes in to the "merry" sounds as he "laugh[s] away care," the second stanza of the poem suggests his aging, and thus his experience of life, which might subtly trouble the innocence of the green. To show my point, I might quote the first five lines of the second stanza, though I might then find myself drifting from the close attention required in a solid analysis. If I take that chance of inattention, I would indent each line ten spaces and reproduce the lines of the poem just as they appear in the text. I would do this because I am quoting four or more lines of poetry. So the quotation would look like this:

> Old John with white hair
>
> Does laugh away care,
>
> Sitting under the oak,
>
> Among the old folk.
>
> They laugh at our play, . . .

After this, I had better make some particular observations about the language of the excerpt that I just quoted.

Remember, your essay's title is not the same as the title of the work you discuss in the essay. Your title has no quotation marks unless you have a quotation in it; neither is it underlined. Use quotation marks for the title of a short poem, essay, or short story. Italicize (or underline) the title of a book, a play, or a long poem—Wordsworth's *Prelude*, for instance.

In quoting prose, if the quotation takes up more than three lines of your text, you should indent the entire block ten spaces. Do not use ellipses (three periods separated by spaces) at the beginning or the end of the quotation; use them in the middle of the quotation to indicate you have removed words that are not essential to your point. Be sure to introduce all quotations with appropriate tags, blending quotations into your own sentence structure, grammar, and syntax. Punctuate quotations and cite page numbers as I do in the following sentence: DuBois begins his essay by depicting and defining the internalized "contempt and pity" of African-American "double-consciousness" (38); he ends the essay by turning that contempt and pity back upon the white America, a "dusty desert of dollars and smartness" (43). Notice that the end punctuation follows the page citation and is not within the quotation itself. Notice also that only the page number is within the parentheses. I would include an author's name only if the particular author was not clear from context.

If you have further questions about MLA style, look in the library for a copy of the *MLA Handbook for Writers of Research Papers,* use a writing handbook such as the Excellence in Literature *Handbook for Writers*, or visit the website below.

https://owl.english.purdue.edu/owl/resource/747/01/

Note: *This sample essay was provided courtesy of Dr. Robert Grotjohn, Professor Emeritus of English, Mary Baldwin College. It was one of the most helpful documents I received while in college, and I used it as a model for nearly every essay I wrote. I hope you find it equally helpful.*

How to Evaluate Writing

"You can always edit a bad page. You can't edit a blank page."

—Jodi Picoult

Grading papers is usually not a favorite chore, but have you ever thought of writing evaluation as a teaching tool? That is exactly what it can be! Every writing assignment and every evaluation can help a student grow as a writer, as long as the standards are clear and the evaluation is constructive and designed to teach. In addition, good evaluations help your student learn how to self-evaluate, which is a skill they will need in college and beyond.

A Constructive Evaluation Starts With a Rubric

What is a rubric? It's a checklist of objective standards. For a student, a rubric defines exactly what the teacher or writing mentor will be checking. Each item on the checklist is a clue as to how to meet the standard. For example, the first Content standard on the EIL rubric is "The essay contains a strong, easily identified thesis." This is a reminder to make sure this is true before you turn in the essay.

For parents and teachers, the rubric outlines what to check in three primary areas: Content (Ideas/Concepts and Organization) first, then Style (Voice, Sentence Fluency, and Word Choice), and finally, Mechanics (Conventions and Presentation). In each of these areas there are three or four specific goals or standards. Your job is to see how well your student meets these standards in each area.

Evaluation Priorities

When medics respond to a disaster with a large number of casualties, they "tri-age" or assign a level of urgency to each problem in order to know what to treat first. In a similar way, it makes sense to evaluate standards in order of importance. One way to think about it is to consider whether the most important part of a paper is WHAT is said, or HOW it is said, or whether everything is spelled correctly.

Because *what* the paper says is of first importance (if the ideas are muddled and illogically organized, all the style and perfect spelling in the world doesn't really matter), begin with Content standards, which evaluate Ideas/Concepts and Organization.

Next, look at *how* the ideas are communicated, including the Style standards of Voice, Sentence Fluency, and Word Choice. Finally, once the content, organization, and general style standards have reached an acceptable level, it will be time to focus on the standards of Mechanics, including grammar, presentation, and so forth.

If a student has many significant areas of difficulty, evaluate only the skills that have been specifically taught, and focus on only a few of the main items in each essay.

Parent Tip: How to Use a Writer's Handbook in Evaluation

A good writer's handbook makes it easy to offer specific, constructive feedback. If you have used a handbook such as the Excellence in Literature *Handbook for Writers*, you know that information is categorized into numbered paragraphs. These numbers allow you to direct the student to exactly the instruction he or she needs to fix an error or improve a skill.

For example, if your student is having difficulty with subject/verb agreement, you would look in the table of contents of the *Handbook for Writers* and find that subject/verb agreement appears in section 4.8 on page 242.

> **1.8 Subject/Verb Agreement**
>
> In any clause, the subject must agree with the verb; that is, a singular subject has a singular verb, and a plural subject has a plural verb. Make sure you do not become confused by some word between the subject and the verb. Notice the following examples.
>
> *The collection of fifty guns has been stolen.*
>
> [The subject is "collection."]
>
> *The disease which infected the trees is root rot.*
>
> [The subject is "disease."]

On the student's paper, underline the incorrect subject/verb combination and note the handbook section number in the margin. When you return the paper, the student should visit the handbook, read the assigned instructional paragraph, look at the examples, and see how to correct the error. Giving feedback this way is quick and efficient, and best of all, so much more helpful than just telling the student to be sure that the subject and verb agree.

How to Evaluate the First Draft

First draft priorities: Ideas/Concepts and Organization

After you do an initial read-through of the student's rough draft, get your writer's handbook and a copy of the rubric and evaluate the two Content skills, Ideas/Concepts and Organization.

I realize it is counter-intuitive for many parents to evaluate only the Content standards, because you will see mechanical errors or style problems in the rough draft. However, until the content and organization of the piece are finalized, there is little point in tweaking word choice or sentence fluency. Working at first with just the content helps keep attention on the first draft priorities of ideas and organization, and avoids the distraction of too much red ink.

How to Evaluate a Final Draft

Final draft priorities: Content, Style, and Mechanics (all standards)

When you receive a revised draft, read through it quickly to gain an overall impression. Have the changes you discussed in the previous draft been satisfactorily made? Use a fresh copy of the rubric to assess each of the seven skill areas and provide a feedback number or symbol for each characteristic listed.

For each draft, return the student's paper with a filled-out rubric, a brief note highlighting the positive and negative things you noticed about the paper, and handbook section numbers so the student can look up challenging items.

Should You Require More than Two Drafts?

Two drafts—a first and a final—are all I recommend. Writing skills improve with each new assignment, and moving through the assignments in a timely manner ensures that students will not get bogged down and end up disliking one of the classics or skipping the last few assignments of the year.

This section adapted from *Evaluate Writing the Easy Way* by Janice Campbell.

Excellence in Literature Evaluation Rubric

Name:	Date:
Assignment:	Evaluator:

Content: Ideas and Concepts _ The essay contains a strong, easily identified thesis. _ Interesting ideas and a compelling perspective hold the reader's attention. _ Relevant anecdotes, appropriate quotes, and specific details support the writer's position and demonstrate understanding of the prompt.	**Content: Organization** _ The structure of the paper enhances the presentation of the thesis and supporting ideas. _ Clear transitions move the reader easily from idea to idea. _ Quotes and textual support are blended smoothly, with correct tenses and formatting.
Style: Voice _ The writer speaks directly to the reader, using an appropriate tone and level of formality. _ The writer's voice is individual and engaging, providing a sense of the writer's personality. _ The writer demonstrates awareness of and respect for the audience and purpose of the writing.	**Mechanics: Conventions** _ Standard writing conventions (spelling, punctuation, capitalization, grammar, usage, paragraphing) are observed. _ Citations are correctly formatted using the MLA standard. _ Mechanical or typographical errors are few; only minor touch-ups needed.
Style: Sentence Fluency _ Sentences flow easily with graceful transitions. _ Sentences have a pleasant, appropriate rhythm and cadence when read aloud. _ Sentence structure is varied, with appropriate use of simple, complex, and compound sentences.	**Mechanics: Presentation** _ Essay is in MLA format: Times-New Roman font, 12 pt., 1″ margins. _ Paper header with student, class, instructor, and date included. _ Essay prompt included after header and before title. _ Single space following all terminal punctuation.
Style: Word Choice _ Chosen words clearly convey the intended message. _ The words used are precise, interesting, powerful, engaging, and natural. _ The vocabulary is vivid and varied, though not necessarily exotic.	**Comments and Handbook Lookups**

Rating Scale

❏ 5 or + indicates that your essay demonstrated outstanding mastery in this area.
❏ 4 indicates that the essay is above average.
❏ 3 or = indicates that your essay was average and met assignment expectations in this area.
❏ 2 indicates that your essay was below average in this area.
❏ 1 or - indicates that you should write down this skill as a goal area for improvement.

Note: This rubric is intended for evaluation of the Week 3/4 assignments only. The shorter assignments from Weeks 1 and 2 are simply checked off on the pacing charts at the front of the book when each assignment is satisfactorily completed.

Excellence in Literature: Student Evaluation Summary

Student: **School Year:**

Grade: **English IV: British Literature**

	Ideas/ Concepts	Organiza- tion	Voice	Word Choice	Sentence Fluency	Mechanics	Presen- tation	Total
Module 4.1- Beowulf								
Module 4.2- Chaucer								
Module 4.3- Gawain & Spenser								
Module 4.4- Shakespeare								
Module 4.5- Milton								
Module 4.6- Austen								
Module 4.7- Dickens								
Module 4.8- Bronte								
Module 4.9- Woolf								
Total								
Average								

Class Description

British Literature is a college-preparatory literature and composition course. Focus works, including novels, short stories, poetry, and drama have been selected for literary quality and for their place in the historic development of literature.

Context readings provide background information about the author, and historic, literary, and artistic context of the focus work. Students will practice the skills of close literary analysis through essays, approach papers, and other types of writing.

Course Objectives

By the end of the course, students will:

- Understand the process of writing, including the use of tools such as a writer's handbook, dictionary, and thesaurus.

- Have specific understanding of selected representative texts by major authors of the periods studied.

- Have a general understanding of the historical and cultural contexts of the works.

- Be able to analyze literary texts and present thoughtfully developed ideas in writing.

- Demonstrate competence in essay organization, style, and mechanics.

- Demonstrate competence in the MLA style of source documentation.

Evaluations

Student writing is evaluated using the Excellence in Writing evaluation rubric. Each paper is analyzed and evaluated in the following seven areas: Ideas and Concepts, Organization, Voice, Word Choice, Sentence Fluency, Mechanics, and Presentation. Course grade is based upon essays (65%), shorter assignments (20%), English and Vocabulary Notebook (10%), and studentship (5%).

Comments

Glossary

*"The difference between the almost right word and the right word is really a large matter—
it's the difference between the lightning bug and the lightning."*

Mark Twain

Allegory: A story in which ideas are represented or personified as actions, people, or things. Example: *Pilgrim's Progress* by John Bunyan.

Alliteration: The repetition of beginning consonant sounds through a sequence of words. Gerard Manley Hopkins is noted for using alliteration in lines such as "Fresh-firecoal chestnut-falls; finches' wings;" from "Pied Beauty."

Allude/Allusion: To make a reference, either implied or stated, to the Bible, mythology, literature, art, music, or history that relies on the reader's familiarity with the alluded-to work to make or reinforce a point in the current work.

Analogy: A comparison based upon similarities and relationships of things that are somewhat alike but mostly different. An analogy often makes a point-by-point comparison from a familiar object to an unfamiliar.

Antagonist: The character who opposes the main character (the protagonist).

Antithesis: A counter-proposition that denotes a direct contrast to the original proposition, balancing an argument for parallel structure.

Excellence in Literature: Reading and Writing through the Classics

Archetype: A plot pattern, such as the quest or the redeemer/scapegoat, or character element, such as the cruel stepmother, that recurs across cultures.

Argument: The reasons (claim, supporting points, and evidence) a writer provides in order to persuade a reader that an idea or thesis is correct.

Assonance: The repetition of vowel sounds in a series of words. Example: "The rain in Spain falls mainly on the plain" from *Pygmalion* by George Bernard Shaw.

Ballad: A narrative poem or song with a repeating refrain. A ballad often tells the story of a historical event or retells a folk legend. Example: "The Raven" by Edgar Allen Poe.

Beast Fable: Also known as a "beast epic," this is an often satirical, allegorical style in which the main characters are animals. It is often written as a mock epic. Example: *Animal Farm* by George Orwell.

Blank Verse: Poetry with regular, metrical, unrhymed lines, usually iambic pentameter.

Burlesque: Refers to ridiculous exaggeration in language, usually one that makes the discrepancy between the words and the situation or the character silly. For example, to have a king speak like an idiot or a workman speak like a king (especially, say, in blank verse) is burlesque. Similarly, a very serious situation can be burlesqued by having the characters in it speak or behave in ridiculously inappropriate ways. In other words, burlesque creates a large gap between the situation or the characters and the style with which they speak or act out the event.

Caricature: The technique of exaggerating for comic and satiric effect one particular feature of a subject, in order to achieve a grotesque or ridiculous effect. Caricatures can be created either through words or pictures.

Characterization: The artistic presentation of a fictional character.

Citation: A standardized reference to a source of information in a written work. The citation usually includes author, title, publisher, and so forth, in a specific format. In the MLA style of citation that we use with this curriculum, the citations appear as signal phrases in the body of the text, and a "works cited" list follows the text.

Climax: The turning point in fiction; the transition from rising to falling action.

Comedy: In literary terms a comedy is a story, often centered on love, that has a positive ending. It may or may not be humorous.

Conflict: A struggle between two opposing forces. The conflict usually forms the central drama in a fictional narrative, and can be man vs. man, man vs. God, man vs. nature, man vs. society, or even man vs. himself.

Consonance: An "almost rhyme" in which consonants agree, but the vowels that precede them differ. Example: word/lord, slip/slop.

Context: In EIL, the conditions and/or circumstances within which a work of literature has been created, including historical events, literary periods, artistic movements, etc.

Couplet: In poetry, a pair of rhyming lines often appearing at the end of a sonnet.

Denouement: Resolution or conclusion.

Diction: An author's word choices.

Didactic: Literature with a moralistic or instructive purpose.

Dystopian: A literary genre featuring a society, often but not always in the future, that is caused and/or characterized by profoundly negative things such as dehumanization, environmental disaster, societal decline, or tyranny. Dystopia is an antonym for utopia.

Elegy: A poem, usually written as a formal lament on the death of a person. In classical time an elegy was any poem written in elegiac meter. Example: "In Memory of W. B. Yeats" by W. H. Auden.

End Rhyme: The repetition of identical or similar sounds in two or more different words found at the end of poetic lines.

Epic: A long narrative poem that tells a story, usually about the deeds of a hero. Example: Beowulf.

Epigram: A brief saying or poem, often ironic or satirical.

Epigraph: A phrase, quotation, or poem that suggests something about the theme and is set at the beginning of a chapter or book.

Episodic fiction: A story composed at loosely connected episodes, usually centering on a central character or group of characters.

Epistolary Style: A novel composed of a series of letters.

Essay: A paper that takes a position on a topic.

Euphemism: The substitution of a socially acceptable word or expression in place of harsh or unacceptable language. Example: "Passed away" for "died."

Exposition: The part of the narrative structure in which the scene is set, characters introduced, and the situation established. It usually falls at the beginning of the book, but additional exposition is often scattered throughout the work.

Fable: A short story, usually featuring animals or other non-human characters, that illustrates a moral lesson. Example: Aesop's "The Crow and the Pitcher."

Falling Action: The portion of plot structure, usually following the climax, in which the problems encountered during the rising action are solved.

Figure of Speech: An intentional deviation from ordinary language use in order to produce an artistic or rhetorical effect. See Scheme and Trope.

Flashback: A plot device in which a scene from the fictional past is brought into the fictional present, often to explain or illustrate a character's next action.

Foot: A group of syllables that form a basic unit of poetic rhythm.

Foreshadow: Hints or clues about future events in a narrative.

Framed Narrative: A story or stories told within a narrative frame. Example: *The Canterbury Tales* by Geoffrey Chaucer. Chaucer has framed a vivid grouping of stories within the frame of a narrative about a group of pilgrims who are traveling to Canterbury.

Free Verse: Poetry that does not rhyme, has no set line length, and is not set to traditional meter.

Full Stop: A period or other punctuation mark that indicates the end of a sentence.

Genre: A category of classification for literature such as fiction, non-fiction, and so forth. Pronounced zhahn-ruh.

Gothic Novel: A genre that evokes an aura of mystery and may include ghosts, dark and stormy nights, isolated castles, and supernatural happenings. Example: *Wuthering Heights* by Emily Brontë or *Frankenstein* by Mary Shelley.

Handbook: A writer's handbook such as the *Handbook for Writers* from Excellence in Literature, *Write for College, Writer's Inc.* from Write Source, or *Writer's Reference* by Diana Hacker.

Heroic Couplet: Two rhymed lines in iambic pentameter, forming a complete thought. This form was often used by Alexander Pope.

Homonym/Homophone: Words that sound much the same but have different meanings, origins, or spelling.

Hubris: A term derived from the Greek language that means excessive pride. In Greek tragedy and mythology, hubris often leads to the hero's downfall.

Hyperbole: Overstatement through exaggerated language.

Imagery: Words, phrases, and sensory details used to create a mood or mental picture in a reader's mind. Example: From "Mariana" by Alfred, Lord Tennyson:
"With blackest moss the flower-plots
Were thickly crusted, one and all;
The rusted nails fell from the knots
That held the pear to the gable wall.
The broken sheds looked sad and strange:
Unlifted was the clinking latch;
Weeded and worth the ancient thatch
Upon the lonely moated grange . . . "

Iambic Pentameter: In poetry, a metrical pattern in a ten-syllable line of verse in which five unaccented syllables alternate with five accented syllables, with the accent usually falling on the second of each pair of syllables.

Irony: A stylistic device or figure of speech in which the real meaning of the words is different from (and opposite to) the literal meaning. Irony, unlike sarcasm, tends to be ambiguous, bringing two contrasting meanings into play.

Literary Device:

Manners: A novel of manners focuses on and describes in detail the social customs and habits of a particular social group. Examples include *Pride and Prejudice* by Jane Austen and *Age of Innocence* by Edith Wharton.

Metaphor: A comparison between two objects, not using the terms "like" or "as."

Meter: The pattern of stressed and unstressed syllables in a line of poetry.

Mock Heroic: A satiric style which sets up a deliberately disproportionate and witty distance between the elevated language used to describe an action or event and the triviality or foolishness of the action (using, for example, the language of epics to describe a tea party). The mock heroic style tends to be an inside joke, in that it appeals to the sophistication of a reader familiar with the epic original but is not understood by readers who are not familiar with the traditional epic form. It encourages the reader to see the ridiculousness of the heroic pretensions of trivial people and is thus an excellent vehicle for skewering the sin of pride. Example: "Mac Flecknoe" by John Dryden or Pope's "Rape of the Lock."

Motif: A recurrent device, formula, or situation, often connecting a fresh idea with common patterns of existing thought.

Myth: A type of story that is usually symbolic and extensive, including stories shared across a culture to explain its history and traditions. Example: "Romulus and Remus."

Narrator: The character who tells the story. This may or may not be the hero, and the narrator may be reliable (trustworthy) or unreliable. Example: Ishmael in *Moby Dick*.

Nature: As it refers to a person, this is used to identify something inborn or inherent, e. g. "human nature" that often leads to predictable actions.

Octave: In poetry, the first eight lines of the Italian, or Petrarchan, sonnet.

Ode: A lyric poem with a serious topic and formal tone but without formal pattern. This form was especially popular among the Romantic poets. Example: "Ode to the West Wind" by Percy Bysshe Shelley.

Omniscient Point of View: In literature, a narrative perspective from multiple points of view that gives the reader access to the thoughts of all the characters.

Onomatopoeia: The formation or use of a word that sounds like what it means. Example: hiss; sizzle; pop.

Oxymoron: A figure of speech that combines two seemingly contradictory elements. Example: living death; sweet sorrow.

Parable: A short story with an explicit moral lesson. Example: The parable of the sower (Matthew 13:18–30).

Paradox: A statement that may appear contradictory but is actually true. Example: "Less is more."

Parody: A style of writing that deliberately seeks to ridicule another style, primarily through exaggeration.

Pastoral: Poem or play that describes an idealized, simple life that country folk, usually shepherds, are imagined to live in a world full of beauty, music, and love.

Personification: To endow a non-human object with human qualities. Example: Death in "Death Be Not Proud" by John Donne.

Picaresque: A style of novel that features a loosely connected series of events, rather than a tightly constructed plot, often with a non-traditional hero. Example: *Moll Flanders* by Daniel Defoe.

Plagiarism: To plagiarize is to copy or borrow the work or ideas of another author without acknowledgment. It is both unethical and illegal. When you are writing anything, such as essays, reports, dissertations, or creative works, you must cite your sources of information, including books, periodicals, or online resources, within your text as well as in a list of references appended to the work.

Plot: The sequence of narrated events that form a story.

Poetic Justice: A literary device in which virtue is ultimately rewarded or vice punished.

Point of View: The perspective from which people, events, and other details in a story are viewed.

Protagonist: The main character in a work, either male or female.

Pseudonym: A false name used to disguise a writer's identity. Example: Mary Anne Evans used the pseudonym George Eliot.

Pun: A wordplay that exploits the double meaning or ambiguity in a word to create an amusing effect. Example: The title of *The Importance of Being Earnest* by Oscar Wilde.

Quest: A type of literary plot that focuses on a protagonist's journey toward a difficult goal. There may or may not be a physical journey involved. Example: Homer's *Odyssey*; J. R. R. Tolkien's *The Lord of the Rings*.

Realism: A type of literature that tries to present life as it really is.

Reductio ad absurdum: A popular satiric technique in which the author agrees enthusiastically with the basic attitudes or assumptions he wishes to satirize and, by pushing them to a logically ridiculous extreme, exposes the foolishness of the original attitudes and assumptions. Example: "A Modest Proposal" by Jonathan Swift.

Refrain: A phrase, line, or group of lines that is repeated throughout a poem, usually after every stanza.

Regional literature: Fiction or poetry that emphasizes setting through colorful details, including dialect, dress, customs, landscape features, and history, of a specific, often rural, place and the people who inhabit it.

Reliable narrator: See "Narrator."

Resolution: The point of closure to the conflict in the plot.

Rhetoric: The art of using language to persuade or influence others. Sometimes includes the idea of eloquence (an older meaning) or of insincerity or artificiality in language (more modern interpretation). Examples: Mark Antony's speech in *Julius Caesar* by William Shakespeare or the character of Squealer in *Animal Farm* by George Orwell.

Rhyme Scheme: The pattern of end rhymes in a poem, noted by small letters, e.g., abab or abcba, etc.

Rising Action: The part of the plot structure in which events complicate or intensify the conflict, or introduce additional conflict.

Romance: A type of novel that presents an idealized picture of life. A novel of romance can be considered almost the opposite of a novel of realism. If you were expecting that the definition of "romance" would have something to do with love, you may want to look at the definition of "comedy" instead.

Rubric: A checklist for scoring that includes guidelines for expectations.

Sarcasm: A form of verbal irony in which apparent praise is actually criticism. Example: "A modest little person, with much to be modest about." Winston Churchill

Satire: A composition in verse or prose that uses humor, irony, sarcasm, or ridicule to point out vice or folly in order to expose, discourage, and change morally offensive attitudes or behaviors. It has been aptly described as an attack with a smile. Example: "A Modest Proposal" by Jonathan Swift.

Scansion: The process of analytically scanning a poem line by line to determine its meter.

Scheme: A rhetorical device or figure of speech in which words or phrases are put together in a manner that is different in syntax, sequence, or pattern from ordinary usage. Example: alliteration, in which a series of words features repetition of consonant sounds, e. g. "And churlish chiding of the winter's wind/ Which, when it bites and blows upon my body" from *As You Like It* by William Shakespeare.

Setting: The time and place in which the action of a story, poem, or play takes place.

Simile: A comparison of two things, using the words "like" or "as." Example: "My love is like a red, red rose . . . " by Robert Burns.

Soliloquy: A monologue in which a character talks to himself. Example: Hamlet's "To be or not to be . . . " soliloquy.

Sonnet: A fixed verse form consisting of fourteen lines, usually in iambic pentameter. Variations include Italian (Petrarchan), Shakespearean, and Spenserian.

Stanza: A section of a poem, preceded and followed by an extra line space.

Stereotype: A characterization based on the assumption that a personal trait such as gender, age, ethnic or national identity, religion, occupation, or marital status is predictably accompanied by certain characteristics, actions, even values.

Stock Character: A flat character sketch that fills a classic, easily understood role without much detail. Example: The wicked stepmother in *Cinderella*.

Stream of Consciousness: A modern writing style that replicates and records the random flow of thoughts, emotions, memories, and associations as they rush through a character's mind. Example: *To the Lighthouse* by Virginia Woolf.

Structure: The arrangement of the various elements in a work.

Style: A distinctive manner of expression distinguished by the writer's diction, rhythm, imagery, and so on.

Summary titles: A style of title in which the author offers a mini preview of the events of the chapter. Usually one sentence in length; often begins with "In which . . .".

Syllabus: An outline of course requirements. In *Excellence in Literature*, the syllabus is this book in its entirety.

Symbol: A person, place, thing, event, or pattern in a literary work that is not only itself but also stands for something else, often something more abstract. Common symbolism includes darkness as a representation of confusion or evil; a storm as foreboding or a threat; or beauty as a symbol of virtue. This PDF may help you understand symbols: http://goo.gl/gGLU4O

Syntax: The rules of grammar and style that govern the arrangement of words and phrases in order to create well-structured sentences.

Textual Support: Brief quotes from a text that is being analyzed. These quotes should usually be smoothly integrated into an original, analytical sentence.

Theme: The main idea or dominant concern of a novel, play, or poem stated in a generalized, abstract way. Example: "Crime does not pay." "Honesty is the best policy."

Thesis: A sentence or statement that summarizes the main idea of any argument and the premise or position that you are arguing.

Tone: The attitude a novel or poem takes toward its subject.

Tragedy: A story in which the character begins at a high point but ends badly, often because of a fatal flaw in his character that causes him to make poor choices. Example: *King Lear* by William Shakespeare; *Oedipus Rex* by Sophocles.

Tragic Flaw: An error in judgment, accidental wrongdoing, or unwitting mistake that results in tragedy, derived from the Greek idea of *hamartia*, or missing the mark.

Tragic Hero: A character, often a noble person of high rank, who comes to a disastrous end in his or her confrontation with a superior force (fortune, the gods, social forces, universal values), but also comes to understand the meaning of his or her deeds and to accept an appropriate punishment.

Trope: A rhetorical device or figure of speech using a word or phrase that intentionally deviates from ordinary language. A metaphor is an example of a trope, as it describes an object or event as something that it clearly is not, in order to make a comparison. Example: "All the world's a stage."

Unreliable Narrator: A speaker or voice whose narration is consciously or unconsciously deceiving. This type of narration is often subtly undermined by details in the story or through inconsistencies with general knowledge.

Voice: The style, personality, and tone of a narrative; also the speaker or narrator. An appropriate voice captures the correct level of formality, social distance, and personality for the purpose of the writing and the audience.

Use the space below to record additional words and definitions you want to remember.

Selected Resources

There is an endless supply of books on reading, writing, and literature, but it can be difficult to find the best. As I look at my bookshelves, I see that many books boast an array of sticky-note flags. When I open them, I find extensive marginal notations, underlined passages, and occasionally, extra slips of paper left at especially important spots. Here are just a few of the well-thumbed volumes on my bookshelves, as well as a few e-resources you will find helpful.

NOTE: Although a few of these optional resources include a faith-based perspective, it is important to note that the Excellence in Literature curriculum approaches literature from a nonsectarian literary perspective. It is designed for use in any teaching setting.

A CiRCE Guide to Reading: This compact guide teaches a multi-layered, flexible approach to reading that includes elements of speed-reading, close reading, and humane reading.

Adventures in Art by David and Shirley Quine: This interactive e-text is designed to help you "visualize the significant changes in ideas throughout history, and then relate those changes to their cultural meaning."

American Passages: A Literary Survey: This well-organized site, designed to enhance the study of American literature, offers timelines, art, and other context information in an easily navigated format. One unique feature allows students to construct a multimedia slideshow of selected materials from the site; then use the slideshow for a presentation.

https://www.learner.org/series/american-passages-a-literary-survey/

"**Analyzing Poetry**" from Study Guide: http://www.studyguide.org/poetry_tips.htm

An Experiment in Criticism by C. S. Lewis: This is my top recommendation for a book on how to approach literature. In less than 150 pages, Lewis explains how to read various types of literature, and incidentally manages to offer hints on approaching music and art as well. Even though this is short, it is rich and well worth reading and re-reading.

Benét's Reader's Encyclopedia: This wonderful resource is described as "the classic and only encyclopedia of world literature in a single volume including poets, playwrights, novelists, and belletrists, synopses, historical data, major characters, in literature, myths and legends, literary terms, artistic movements, and prize winners." Any of the older editions will include the important elements of the Western literary tradition. I use it often.

The Company of the Creative: A Christian Reader's Guide to Great Literature and Its Themes by David L. Larson: This helpful, nonsectarian guide offers brief overviews of great authors and their work, plus useful recommendations for further reading.

Developing Linguistic Patterns Through Poetry Memorization by Andrew Pudewa: To write well, a student needs to internalize the rhythm and cadence of well-composed language. This book will help you accomplish that.

A Dictionary of Literary Symbols by Michael Ferber: This helpful guide, now available free online, "explains . . . literary symbols that we all frequently encounter (such as swan, rose, moon, gold), and gives hundreds of cross-references and quotations" from classic authors, the Bible, and English, American, and European literature.

https://www.academia.edu/37950209/Michael_Ferber_A_Dictionary_of_Literary_Symbols_Cambridge_University_Press_1999_pdf

Discovering Music: Dr. Carol Reynolds has created a "unique curriculum [that] takes you through the history of music, the arts, and Western Culture from 1600 to

1914" in about 13 hours of video instruction. This is an excellent context supplement to EIL. http://discoveringmusic.net/

The Elegant Essay Writing Lessons: Building Blocks for Analytical Writing by Lesha Myers: If a student needs extra help in essay writing, this simple guide can help. This may be used before or concurrently with Excellence in Literature.

Excellence-in-Literature.com: Here you will find many of the context resources and study references used in the *Excellence in Literature* curriculum and *Model-Based Writing*.

Excellence in Literature *Handbook for Writers*: The first half of this 400+ page handbook for student and teacher contains detailed instruction on essay writing, including a selection of sample outlines for different types of papers. The second half is a guide to usage and style, including sentence construction, word usage, punctuation, and more.

Gutenberg: Free Books: This wonderful site contains many classic books in digital form. I don't recommend reading on a screen unless you have to, but these book files might be useful if you cannot find a copy locally.

How to Read a Book: The Classic Guide to Intelligent Reading by Mortimer J. Adler and Charles Van Doren: There are multiple levels of reading—elementary, inspectional, and synoptical—and the authors clearly explain each and teach the reader how to appropriately read various types of literature.

How to Read and Why by Harold Bloom: A Yale professor and author of many books on literature, Bloom offers this brief volume of selections chosen not "as an exclusive list of what to read, but rather a sampling of works that best illustrate why to read." For a more extensive overview of the classics, you may want to read The Western Canon.

How to Read Slowly: Reading for Comprehension by James W. Sire: This is a concise introduction (just six chapters!) to reading literature from a worldview perspective.

Imitations in Writing: The Grammar of Poetry by Matt Whiting: This accessible text "focuses on teaching the fundamentals of poetry (figurative language, meter, rhyme, etc.) by means of imitation and review." We found it to be an easy-to-use introduction to poetry.

Invitation to the Classics: A Guide to Books You have Always Wanted to Read by Louise Cowan and Os Guinness: This attractive guide presents a chronological survey of great literature. The purpose of the book is to "introduce the Western literary masterworks in a clear and simple style that is mature in seriousness and tone and Christian in perspective—and in doing so, to help reawaken Western people to the vibrant heritage of these classics that are rich in themselves and in their two-thousand-year relationship to the Christian faith."

Librivox: Free Audio Books: The exciting thing about LibriVox is that you do not have to be content with just the books they offer—you can record and upload your own! The quality of these amateur recordings varies, but the price is right. http://librivox.org/

The Lifetime Reading Plan by Clifton Fadiman: Fadiman offers an overview of the Western canon, with brief discussions about each author and his or her greatest works. His aim is to help the reader "avoid mental bankruptcy" and to "understand something …of our position in space and time …[and] know how we got the ideas by which …we live."

Norton Anthologies: I recommend looking for used copies of the Norton Anthologies at used bookstores, remainder tables, or online, because they contain decent author introductions and their chronological format makes it easy to see the literary context of the works we will study throughout Excellence in Literature. Other anthologies may be useful, but I like the older Norton editions because they tend to stick with the classics. I suggest getting the American, English, World, and Poetry anthologies.

Writing About Literature: Norton's basic instruction in how to read analytically and write an analytical essay. This resource seems to move regularly. If this link does not work, try doing a web search for "Writing About Literature: Norton," and you may find it.

https://wwnorton.com/college/english/write/writesite/rhetoric/writing_about_lit.aspx

On Writing Well: An Informal Guide to Writing Nonfiction by William Zinsser- There is a good reason that this classic resource just celebrated its thirtieth anniversary with a new edition; it is an excellent model for its subject. Zinsser begins with an overview of writing principles, then moves into detailed discussion of forms and methods. It is a valuable resource for any writer.

The Politically Incorrect Guide to English and American Literature by Elizabeth Kantor, Ph.D. is an entertaining romp through selected English language literature. Overall, the book provides a memorable introduction to the ideas that have shaped the literary world, as well as sound recommendations for books you must not miss (most of them are included in the Excellence in Literature series).

Reading Between the Lines: A Christian Guide to Literature by Gene Edward Veith, Jr.: This interesting guide begins with a chapter on the importance of reading, then progresses through the forms, modes, and traditions of literature, with extensive end-notes for each chapter.

Vocabulary Study: If you enjoy vocabulary study and would like to add a vocabulary program to the contextual vocabulary study in EIL, Dynamic Literacy's W*ord Build* program goes beyond the simple study of roots by using "morphology, the study of the units of meaning in words. [Just as] mastery of phonics helps students 'sound out' unfamiliar words; a mastery of morphics helps students 'mean out' unfamiliar words." An alternative is the *Vocabulary from Classical Roots* series, which presents Greek and Latin roots in a series of well-designed lessons.

Write for College: A Student Handbook: Specific instructions on many types of writing, plus a proofreader's guide to grammar, punctuation, and style, and much more. Younger students may prefer *Writer's INC*, which is similar, but for 11th–12th grades and beyond, *Write for College* or the EIL *Handbook for Writers* (referenced earlier) is most useful.

A Writer's Reference by Diana Hacker: I still turn to this brief handbook because of its handy tabbed format and helpful citation guides, including MLA and APA styles. It might be a useful supplement to either of the other suggested guides.

Word Processing Software

If you do not have a full-featured word processing program such as Microsoft Word, I recommend Google's free online suite of applications, including a word processor, spreadsheet program, and other tools. All you need for access to these is a free Google account, available at https://accounts.google.com/SignUp.

About the Author

*The greatest part of a writer's time is spent in reading,
in order to write; a man will turn over half a library to make one book."*

— Samuel Johnson

Janice Campbell, a lifelong reader and writer, loves to introduce students to great books and beautiful writing. She holds an English degree from Mary Baldwin College, and is the graduated homeschool mom of four sons.

Janice speaks at conferences nationwide on subjects including literature, writing, homeschool planning, high school records and transcripts, and other topics for homeschooling families, co-ops, and private schools. She is the author of the *Excellence in Literature* curriculum for grades 8-12, *Transcripts Made Easy*, and *Get a Jump Start on College*, and the publisher of a new edition of the 1857 McGuffey Readers with instructions for use with Charlotte Mason methods. In addition, she is an occasional host on the Homeschool Solutions podcast.

You'll find more of Janice's writing about reading, writing, and education from a Charlotte Mason/Classical perspective in various magazines and at her websites, EverydayEducation.com (the bookstore), Excellence-in-Literature.com (the literature resource site), and DoingWhatMatters.com (the blog). Whether you are homeschooling or teaching in a co-op or classroom, you're sure to find helpful tips and resources on all three sites.

CPSIA information can be obtained
at www.ICGtesting.com
Printed in the USA
BVHW011422090822
644143BV00007B/540